Love and Loss in Cambodia: a memoir
Copyright © Debra Groves Harman 2019

Canby Media
ISBN 978-0-578-53778-8
Published in the USA June 2019

Love and Loss
in
Cambodia
a memoir

Debra Groves Harman

Under the Harvest Moon

Under the harvest moon,
When the soft silver
Drips shimmering
Over the garden nights,
Death, the gray mocker,
Comes and whispers to you
As a beautiful friend
Who remembers.

Under the summer roses
When the flagrant crimson
Lurks in the dusk
Of the wild red leaves,
Love, with little hands,
Comes and touches you
With a thousand memories,
And asks you
Beautiful, unanswerable questions.

~~Carl Sandburg

For Jay

and in memory of my brother Warren, with his blue, blue eyes.

$\mathscr{P}$rologue

The Cambodian students asked if their first assignment could be to write about the Khmer Rouge era.

"Of course, if you want. But you don't have to write about that," I said. "You can write about your families or hobbies."

"It's up to you," said one woman.

"Yes, up to you," said an older man.

The essays were turned in two days later, neatly handwritten with blue or black ink. Never red.

"When someone dies, we wear red, like this," Sokunthea said in class, showing me a red string tied around her wrist. Her grandmother had died the previous week.

"We are sad for 100 days, and after that we eat chicken soup. Then, we are happy." She made it sound so simple, but it was just a language issue. I knew it was more complicated.

That weekend, I sat at the little kitchen table of our apartment on the southern coast of Cambodia, the essays in a stack. Each essay had a family story about the Khmer Rouge years. I read their words:

"My uncle died of starvation. He was very kind. We miss him."

"My family was hungry all the time."

"The Khmer Rouge killed so many people."

"My sister died. I lived."

I wrote sympathetic comments. I sure as hell wasn't going to correct their spelling and grammar. Not on this assignment. Students were optimistic, too:

"I want my family to be healthy and rich."

"I want happy and lucky for all."

With my green pen, I suggested: "I want happiness and luck for all."

I lit a clove cigarette and drank from a bottle of water, then tipped my head back and poured the rest of the water over my forehead, pulling the moisture through my hair with my hands. The water splashed on the tiles and dried in twenty minutes. I put my hair up in a bun and secured it with a bamboo chopstick. My husband liked long hair. In this heat it drove me crazy.

The older students were my age, teenagers during the Khmer Rouge years from 1975 through 1979. I picked up the last essay. Vanny, a ministry official in Cambodia, wrote these words:

"We lived in hell until 1979. The truth. For a long time life is difficult."

In 1979, the final year that the Khmer Rouge created hell on earth for their fellow Cambodians, I struggled to get through a day back in the U.S. I drank too much, smoked like a chimney, and was miserable. At the time, I was only nineteen. That seemed a lifetime ago.

Now it was 1994, fifteen years past the Khmer Rouge era, and the pain of my loss in Oregon. It occurred to me that the Cambodians probably knew how to deal with grief. They had been through so much of it. About two million people in the country had died, close to a third of the population. Moms and dads and brothers and sisters. One my end, I'd only lost one person.

People have asked me time and again how I ended up in Cambodia. I guess it all started back in the 70s when my brother died.

1

$\mathcal{D}$eath

I was nineteen and my brother Warren was eighteen when he died. He end-over-ended his red Malibu after hitting a culvert in the wee hours of June 26th, 1979 three miles from his bed at home. My brother's death nearly killed my parents.

"Don't have an open casket," said the coroner. The head injury had been too violent. My mother cried and walked around the house. Dad and I wandered around the yard with its maple and cedar trees. The June 26th morning rose around us. The sun came up. The birds sang. We cried. It would be a record high day, as the previous day was. Around 5 a.m., Dad got his Jim Beam out of the cupboard and sat in a lawn chair, crying and staring to the east, waiting for the sun to rise over the field of Christmas trees.

Mom cried in the house and made phone calls. I went upstairs into the dark cool attic and found Warren's graduation suit, a powder blue jacket and vest with the light blue slacks. I brought it downstairs and hung it on the door leading to Mom and Dad's room. Mom said, "No, no," and moved it into the closet. My parents knew my heart. I needed a task, a responsibility. I needed to do anything to stay busy. They sent me to fetch Sis in Aloha, twenty miles up the road. I drove nearly blinded by tears, choking and sobbing when I pulled over to get gas. An old gas station attendant with sad eyes pressed a roll of toilet paper into my hand and said, "Honey, take this. Save cryin' for later, but you gotta drive. Come on, here's some tissue. Pull it together. Don't drive when you cryin', you ain't safe."

When we got to the farm, my sister hugged my parents and then went straight to bed. The building might be on fire, but her approach was to bury herself like a tiny seed, deep in bed. When it was time, she emerged. She slept for hours, then days. On the fourth day, she emerged and got ready for the funeral. I had arranged for my best friend Bell to play taps on her trumpet, Lily and her sister to sing with their guitars, and two friends to speak. The honorary pallbearers were ready, and the blue leaflets for the funeral attendees were in the basket, with the sign-in booklet and its fancy pen. Flowers were everywhere. I'd met with the organist and delivered sheet music for

"I'll Follow the Sun" and other modern songs. Funeral home music for kids didn't exist.

The funeral home parking lot filled with teenagers. Muscle cars of the '60s and '70s lined the streets: El Caminos, Ford trucks with candy-apple red paint jobs, Camaros, Mustangs, and Barracudas. Pretty young girls in sexy, black dresses who smelled like musk perfume and Love's Sunny Lemon came in with handsome young men. Somber and red-eyed, they filled the funeral home. Aunts and uncles and cousins sat with us in the veiled side chamber that afforded us privacy. My brother's powder-blue coffin stood at the front, closed. So many flowers crowded before it, pots of pink and yellow and white mums. Grandma on my mom's side was a florist, and my mom's siblings and large family sent white roses, baby white carnations, stargazer lilies, and spikes of white gladiolus.

The service passed like a smoking truck on an uphill climb. I sat in silence. I absorbed the two hours, each word, rustle of suit and silk, the fumble with the tissue box, the emotional vibrato of the trumpet. The girls' thin voices singing. The air heady with roses. My mom's spearmint gum in her purse, two seats away.

The previous night, I drove to the funeral home on Grant Street. The director was there until 9 p.m., he said earlier when we planned the service. I greeted him and asked him to unlock the coffin.

"I can't recommend a viewing," he said. "He had a bad head injury. I'm so sorry." He held up his hands in a "no can do" gesture.

"I'm nineteen," I said. "He's my brother."

The funeral director turned to the coffin, inserting a key into the lock of my brother's casket. He may have done more cosmetic work if he'd known someone would look. Was this a mistake? Suddenly, there he was.

Warren's curly, brown hair, long and wild, framed his face. Why had they parted it in the middle? He wore the powder blue suit. His face was swollen, especially his closed eyes. In life, they'd been light blue, unusually so. His hands were gently placed one atop the other, over his belly. The hands of a mechanic, his fingernails were dark from grease and oil. He worked on his car, and welded at work. I liked it that they couldn't clean his hands. With my index finger, I traced the curve between his finger and his thumb. He was so cold. I pulled back, surprised. I had never touched a dead person. This was my brother, but I wouldn't touch him again. Tears came to my eyes, but dried fast. I didn't blink. I stayed with him for ten more minutes. I was as still as stone.

My mother cried for days after the funeral. People tried to comfort her with the canned phrases. She wasn't in the least soothed, and I tried to shield her from the most offensive of the phrases.

"At least you have the girls."

"He's in a better place now."

"God won't give you anything you can't handle."

Mom was a tipped canoe, and couldn't right herself, walking with her head slightly leaned to one side. She wiped mascara from under her eyes and pressed cold cloths under them to take down the swelling. She no longer sang. Even her irritated words to Dad just stopped. Dad and I worried. We watched.

Mom and Dad both had other love interests, and were planning a divorce. Before my brother died, they shut themselves in their bedroom and argued quietly, or took long walks we watched from the windows inside. This made us kids very anxious. I remember trying to leave the house constantly. I worried constantly my parents would divorce and propel us into chaos. That they were kind to each other after Warren died was oddly peaceful.

Late summer, brown leaves fell early from the big-leaf maples around our farmhouse. Sandy showed up with a friend. They were leaving for Arizona and sunshine. Mom, Dad, and I cheerfully waved her off. They pressed money into her palm. No one blamed her for heading south. Seeing her happy made us glad. We were excited for her.

During my early teen years, my family sat at the table and ate in uncomfortable silence. One night, my parents erupted in anger. Dad picked up his steak knife and stabbed the glossy mahogany table, his eyes wild. Mom threw a wine glass at the wall near his head, and pink chablis dripped down the wall. We kids left the table, shocked, and tiptoed upstairs to our bedrooms.

"This is so wrong!" I whispered.

"It's ridiculous!" my sister said.

"Oh, come on now. It's total fucking bullshit!" my brother said, raising his eyebrows like Groucho Marx.

After Warren died, home became a quiet place. The first year passed, and the grief didn't budge. It settled in like a heavy boulder. Neither parent was a role model for how to grieve. Dad slumped in an old green chair with his feet up on the footstool, his head on his hand. He stared at the TV. Mom made dinner without a word, dabbed on some peach lipstick and Arpège perfume, and announced she was going bowling. She returned around midnight, shutting the front door quietly. She sat in the kitchen and cried.

I went downstairs and put my arm around her, saying, "Mom, Mom. It's okay," although it wasn't. I filled a glass at the sink and shook aspirin from the bottle on the sill. I walked her to bed, stopping at the bathroom to help her wash up. Dad grunted sleepily and rolled on his side. Everyone worked in the morning, so we were up at dawn drinking coffee.

My parents' divorce was imminent, and it happened without much fuss. One day, Mom moved out into an apartment. Soon after the divorce, Mom remarried an unremarkable little man from her workplace, a man with light blue eyes like my brother's. She drank and danced and chattered away with the new husband Dale with blue eyes. She smelled like tobacco and packed around a thermos, something she'd never done.

"Mom," I said, "We should talk. I'm worried about you."

"Oh, I'm doing better now, honey, but thanks for worrying about me," she'd say. Her eyes had dulled. She avoided looking at me. Her soul was not there. Mom walked slowly from room to room, emptying ashtrays and tidying the cheap apartment. This was so unlike our farmhouse in the countryside. I saw empty vodka bottles under the sink. I wondered when this would end. I missed my mom. She was gone.

I thought about Mom's new relationship and figured it out. Her new husband's name was Dale, my brother's middle name. Marrying him—his light blue eyes and his name—was the act of a miserably depressed woman who'd lost her only son. Years later, she admitted this to me.

"I was depressed. It was a mistake," she told me at the County Courthouse, filing divorce papers. "He reminded me of Warren Dale. I could stare at his eyes. I could say his name—Dale, Dale, Dale. But he wasn't Warren Dale."

On the other hand, Dad did okay. His girlfriend Denice, a pretty blonde like Mom, moved in and planted tulips, and worked to merge families. My sister and I weren't thrilled. We took sides, and Dad drew the short straw. We didn't like the newcomer in Mom's kitchen, but Sandy lived in Arizona and Mom was struggling. I didn't have the fight to launch a solo protest. I moved into an apartment with Bell, and tried to avoid the drama. Our lives could only get better, I hoped.

2

*D*estruction

In early 1982, Dad and his girlfriend Denice were in a wreck themselves, so injured that their survivals baffled the doctors. At the apartment, my boyfriend answered the phone and handed it to me. I needed to get to the hospital fast to talk with the trauma surgeon. *Hurry.* I was twenty-two years old. I felt seventy.

Why me? I was a young adult. My friends had careers, relationships, college, and love. Why was I always in crisis with my immediate family? I loved them, so I couldn't turn away, but how was I supposed to handle all of this death, alcoholism, and trauma? This couldn't be normal. It wasn't normal.

Stumbling to my bedroom, I collapsed onto the edge of my bed, sitting down fast. I was so dizzy I could hardly stand, and felt overwhelmed. How could this be happening? First my brother and now this? I stood up, the earth spinning. Nothing made sense. I filled my lungs and exhaled hard. It was time to go to the hospital. Time to be responsible and talk with doctors. My boyfriend drove me to the hospital, where my aunt met me. She left after filling me in.

A car had pulled out in front of Dad on 99E, the same highway where my brother died fewer than three miles south. The "safety corridor" is what highway 99E was called, mostly as a reminder so people turn on their lights and drive carefully. So many people have died on that road. The driver, in an old Impala, didn't even see Dad in his little Dodge Colt.

Later, my best friend Bell said, "Let someone else take a turn! Why do you always have to do *everything*?" There was no one else. My sister was in Arizona, living with a boyfriend who proposed when he heard she was needed back home. Dad's girlfriend was lying in a coma. His mother was in the hospital getting ready for surgery. He'd been on his way to visit her. And his parents were in their late seventies anyway. His sister didn't want to deal with him. She had a life to live.

I was it, and couldn't turn my back. Dad was in the intensive care unit for several months, flown to Emmanuel Hospital in Portland, Oregon, by Life Flight helicopter. The steering wheel crushed his chest and bruised his heart, ripping one lung in two. Air from his lungs filled the space between skin and flesh, "subcutaneous emphysema." He was blown up like a balloon, with a huge belly, and fingers like sausages. His testicles, like grapefruits, lifted the sheets. He was a mess.

A bloody sheet covered Dad's crushed and flattened right leg. His face was bruised and his eyes swollen shut, and blood splattered the white sheets. A tube in his mouth led to a squeezed device held by a nurse. He was being ventilated. When they wheeled him toward the intensive care unit from emergency, he reached for my hand and squeezed it three times, "I love you." How was he even conscious?

Later, Sis flew in from Arizona. We collapsed on small vinyl couches in the ICU waiting room. The Life Flight helicopter pad was just outside, and through the darkened window, we heard the chopper blades, and felt the vibration and landing. The helicopter was unpredictable. Sometimes it landed twice in eight hours, sometimes every other day. We rushed to the window and stared through a dark glass window that didn't open. Emergency crewmembers bustled around. I learned to leave the waiting room as the wailing family members came in. It was all too much. Sis flew back to Arizona after a few weeks, and it was just me.

Against odds, Dad lived, but it was months in the hospital and more than two years of surgeries. Respiratory therapists performed a tracheotomy, and a machine breathed for him for weeks, then months. By the time they took it out, he'd lost seventy pounds. One day, the nurse proudly announced she'd taught him to talk again, by taking a deep breath, covering the hole with his finger, and talking.

"He'll sound normal eventually, but don't be surprised for now. He sounds high and squeaky." Dad lay there, eyes intense in his thin face as he drew a huge breath. I waited for his first words, excited. What would he say?

"This nurse is a total bitch! Get her out of my room!" I was shocked, and apologized. The nurse bustled out fast. Dad seldom used language around me, but he hated it there. Apparently he hated that nurse, too. After his heart and lungs got better, they began working on the crushed leg. It was a mess. The artificial hip surgery went well, but his knee was ruined.

The surgeon offered a choice: amputate it, or fuse it— permanently straight and as hard as an oak log. That's what he chose. After it was fused, he had an external fixator, a large device on his leg that screwed into his leg bones, and a large metal device outside of the leg to hold it straight. The pain was intense, he said. The scabby holes where the screws went through skin and bone seeped, and movement made him gasp in pain. I cleaned the wounds, gently dabbing the perimeter of the ¼ inch holes in his legs with q-tips dipped in hydrogen peroxide. Two years had passed since the accident, and I can't count the surgeries. There were many. I was twenty-four now.

My life had gotten downright depressing. I worked, then took care of Dad. My love life had tanked, and my boyfriend had gotten tired of the hospital scene out at the farm. I didn't know, as a young adult, how to deal with the mess of my dad's injuries. I certainly didn't know how to be a care provider to a parent. And Dad was difficult. He was driving me crazy, and I felt trapped in my family home.

The house smelled like pee, stale sweat, bleach, and Cheez-its. Dad kept the curtains closed to reduce glare on the television screen. I did daily hospital visits, therapy visits, shopped for groceries, washed laundry, paid bills, delivered mail, and spent hours in surgery waiting rooms. My small car had wheelchairs and crutches in the trunk, held closed with bungee cords. I spent months emptying and rinsing urinals, and packing medications in little two-week trays. I argued with insurance companies, "Can you please check again to see if canes or walkers are covered?"

"I'll have to put you on hold. It may take a while." Thirty minutes would pass. I remember slamming the phone so hard I heard a chorus of bells, like angels telling me, *Calm yourself.*

While I'd worked as a nurse's aide in my late teens, I wasn't perfect at it, not with my own father. Some days I encouraged Dad to wheel his own chair around the house, and walk into the bathroom unassisted. If I got impatient, he'd yell, "Why don't you just get the hell out of here?" and I drove away, worried about their dinner and feeling depressed. I needed out. The occupational therapist nearly refused to sign Dad's discharge papers from the hospital the previous year, saying he couldn't live independently, but I pushed to get him home. He'd been in the hospital for so long.

Soon, Denice was there in her wheelchair and crutches. Together, they were healing, and happiness is a good doctor. At nights I served them dinner and ate standing up. I collapsed into bed, setting the digital alarm clock for work the next morning. I cried in frustration. I was exhausted always.

I was ready to move on, and fortunately, Mom was also reclaiming her life. When I knocked on her apartment door to stage a one-person intervention, her blue-eyed little husband proudly told me that she'd checked herself into Serenity Lane or some such place. Later, she invited me to attend a few Alcoholics Anonymous meetings. The AA meetings were new to me.

Mom's twelve-step program included making amends. The conversations were hard, as I was young and her apologies made me sad. One day she was ironing a blouse in the spare bedroom of her apartment. At forty-nine, she was trim and well dressed, with striking green eyes. She quietly said, "I'm sorry for all the mess, for everything." I understood, and I loved her. Still, I felt deserted when my brother died.

"Mom, we should talk about things," I said.

"Look, Deb, I'm trying to apologize," she said. Clearly, she didn't want a dialogue. She was working step nine, and she didn't feel all that comfortable with it. Yet, I had feelings I'd stuffed deep inside, because I missed my family. I missed my brother, my sister who had moved to Arizona, my father who was rendered mute for months with a tracheotomy and breathing machine, and Mom, who now wanted to talk. Sort of. The ground constantly shifted under me, but I couldn't say all that. Mom had her own problems, and didn't need to listen to mine.

She turned off the iron and hung her blouse up, and we went to the little dining room and drank coffee. It was too painful to talk about the last few years. We talked about happy things—my sister and her husband, and Mom's new job. My college plans. We'd look forward, not back. It was easier.

By that time, I'd started making some sense of it all. My brother's death wasn't the cause of the pain. It was the ultimate symptom of our family's dysfunction, a huge red flag that we were broken. When people start dying, it's a sign, right? My brother was the youngest member of our family, and he was gone. It was our fault. I wore this knowledge like a heavy yoke around my neck.

Maybe I should have moved far away, like my sister had. Maybe I should have run from the aftermath of my brother's death. Or maybe I didn't understand it was time to get into a life raft and push away. That's the negative part of my brain talking, though. Mostly, I don't give up on people. If there's the faintest glimmer of life, I'm that person doing CPR for a solid hour. Sometimes I was the one that needed saving, though.

I drank heavily in my early twenties. Whenever I could escape work and checking on my parents, I hiked in the wilderness of Oregon or California somewhere and drank to excess. For the most part, my parents and I were doing better in the mid '80s. President Reagan was in office, Madonna was all over FM radio, and people wore unlaced leather tennis shoes, dramatic mullets, and parachute pants. The AIDS quilt was traveling throughout the states, and I viewed it in Portland, Oregon, writing my high school friend Kody's name on a square. He was the first Oregon person to die of AIDS, that sweet boy who lived down the road from us. I cried for Kody and I cried for Warren.

Several years had passed since my brother's death. My family had suffered tremendously. My father had nearly died in his own car accident. My stepmom, in the accident with him, awoke from her month-long coma to find she had broken both knees and a hand. She had seizures, and her short-term memory was destroyed. My mom quit drinking after she lost her money and her health. I'd suffered too. I mostly stopped drinking when an accident nearly killed me.

Bell and I went to visit a friend. We drank wine and Bell was driving, so I overdid it. I got out of the car and fell like a dead cedar in the Oregon woods. My head struck the cement curb. Friends from our apartment complex carried me into an apartment, and the ambulance came. At the hospital, I cried and told the nurse my brother had died. I reeked of booze, and was a bloody sobbing mess.

The nurse glared at me with raised eyebrows and said, "Better get it together. This one was close." For two weeks, I had black eyes, and initially, they were swollen shut. My face looked like my brother's had when he was lying in the coffin. I had an epiphany: if I kept this up, I'd end up in the ground next to my brother.

How had things gone this far? I quit binge drinking and tried to spend more time with Mom. We became close like we'd been when I was young. Her eyes became clear and brilliant green again, and so did mine. She lost weight. So did I.

Those years in the late '70s and early '80s were high Cascade Mountains we needed to cross to get to the warmth. Mom and I began talking about things that mattered---books, ideas, our jobs. We talked about everything except what really mattered to me. My depression. I couldn't stop thinking about my brother. I didn't talk with her about that, because I knew it could destroy her again.

Unresolved grief hung on. In 1984, doctors weren't yet handing out antidepressants, which I could have used. Depression and mental illness were shushed up back then, so I didn't have any resources. I desperately wanted to fix the mess of my life, to feel joy and hope, to wake up without feeling sad.

Bell invited me to hear Elizabeth Kübler-Ross speak up at Portland State University. She was a death guru, an unconventional Swiss woman who'd come up with a paradigm for coping with death and grief. Could she help me? Bell seemed to think so.

"We're all going to die," she said, "Someone's always going to be left behind."

"I can't stand the thought of living like this forever," I said.

"It'll get better. You just need time," she said

"With the millions of people in the world, I should be able to find someone like my brother," I said. It wasn't just him I'd lost. I'd lost my family. They were either horribly damaged or gone. Not only that, I couldn't talk with them about my grief. That was clear. They were as sad as I was.

So we ended up at Portland State University to hear Kübler-Ross, the death guru. She was an older woman. A packed audience listened intently. She described denial, anger, bargaining, depression, and acceptance. The stages might not occur in that order. They were potential feelings. Originally, the stages applied only to terminally ill people, but later on, she expanded her paradigm to explain emotions of people who grieved. She was on tour, talking to crowds all over the USA.

Years later, I read that Kübler-Ross lost some credibility for conducting sexy séance sessions for widows. A male friend of hers "channeled" their deceased husbands' spirits and copulated with them in the dark, filling the void in their lives. I didn't know this as a naïve twenty-five-year-old. I was optimistic about ditching depression, and longed for the acceptance stage. Kübler-Ross, who was posthumously awarded the "loose screw award" by *Psychology Today* magazine had my full attention.

On the way home, Bell and I talked, rain seeping through the windows of her VW Beetle. It was a constant battle to keep the windshield clear, and I wiped them with *Willamette Week* newspapers as we drove.

"Can you believe how many people she's watched die?" she said.

"A hundred people you don't know isn't as hard as one person you love," I said.

"Oh, stop. Kübler-Ross was talking about little kids dying, and people in concentration camps," Bell said. "Grieving is normal. You'll get through it in your time."

She was right. Time was the only promising vehicle to carry me far away from my brother's death. Kübler-Ross hadn't offered me a quick fix, but time seemed to be helping. I tried hard to focus my mind on ideas and news, which was a distraction from thinking about my brother and my grief. Bell became the closest person in my life. She knew all about depression, because she lived with it too. She didn't mind me being such a wreck. I minded, though.

Grief was like struggling in turbulent seas, wave after wave smacking me in the face. I needed to float, to shut my mouth and hold my breath when a big wave hit. I had to learn how to deal with death. It would happen again, and how would I cope with it? Thinking about the people I loved dying and leaving me behind, a wave of nausea washed through me. I wanted to die before they did. Otherwise, I'd be a broken shell on the beach of life. I had to find a way to withstand grief, to bear it without letting it crush me.

I still carried sadness like a handbag. Still, I began to make sense of what had happened. Warren hadn't meant to die. It was an accident. He hadn't meant to break all our hearts. He'd feel bad if he knew I was unhappy.

Around that time, I went camping with Bell along the Deschutes River. One morning I was shivering uncontrollably. Bell said "You can control this. Let the cold in. Just sit with it. Let it in." I took a deep breath, then another. I noticed the stillness of the sky. The river, opaque and deep blue, moved past with the occasional bird skimming the surface. My breath made small puffs of steam. I calmed myself.

That's what I began doing with my pain, too. I let it in.

3

*L*ife

I worked for the State of Oregon until I was twenty-five, teaching woodworking and body mechanics to injured workers being rehabilitated. The men working in the shop as industrial therapists were unsupportive that I was hired. That's an understatement. Back then, women weren't welcome in the trades. I ran shop equipment, and worked with the clients. Still, it wasn't always very fun. I got harassed, especially the first year.

As the only woman in an all-male workshop environment, I dealt with pencils left on my desk with penis-shaped erasers, a live two-foot garter snake in my desk and a "just in case" sack hung on my office wall, "just in case" the woman someone picked up at a bar's closing time ended up ugly in the morning. The idea was to put the sack on her head as she lay there. Like "beer goggles" people talk about now, the glasses that make prospective mates look more attractive at 2 a.m. when the bar's closing.

The perpetrator was my office partner, Will. He was a close friend of the chief administrator, who hired him. One day, Will whacked me hard on the head with a heavy binder. He was mad about his failing marriage, and unhappy that his sack was missing (it disappeared from the wall, taken down by a sympathetic friend who found it disgusting). Will was sleeping with my best friend Lara, who worked in the main building. He was getting nervous I'd rat him out to his wife.

"Damn it, get out of the office," Will said. "I'm dictating a report and need silence."

"Yeah," I snickered. "I'll leave the office for two hours while you're doing that." Through the window, I saw him tilting back in his chair, smiling as he talked with Lara. I'd go to the main building to deliver wood I'd planed and edged on the shop machines, and see Lara in her office on the phone, smiling. When I walked back to the shop he was still tilted back in his chair, beaming.

"Might be nice to get some of my paperwork done," I said, as he walked out of our office. My male co-workers stood in a circle with me, smirking at Will. They disapproved of the hours he spent on the phone.

"Shut up," he said, and hit me hard with the three-ring binder he was carrying. My head was tender from my concussion two years before, and I felt dizzy. I thought about it for a few days, then marched to the main building and reported him for sexual and physical harassment. Weeks of interviews took place. My officemate Will followed me around the shop.

"Look, I'm a Vietnam War vet. Cut me some slack."

I didn't see the relevance. I ignored him.

"I shouldn't have been rude. I'm sorry!"

I walked away.

"Can you just accept my apology?"

When I complained, the staff in HR told him to leave me alone. I was in my mid twenties, an age when workplace issues are high drama. Finally, the secretary called me in to talk with the administrator. He was a portly man with close-set eyes and the generically boring dark suit. He'd never before spoken to me, but now I sat in his office in jeans and a flannel shirt. I wasn't prepared for this meeting, called without prior warning.

"I'm happy to report that our investigative team has discovered that you *have not* been sexually harassed," he said, in a congratulatory tone of voice. Then, he lectured me for giving "mixed messages" to the all-male staff. The union rep shifted in his seat. Just the week before, my shop supervisor had slid a piece of paper across his desk to me, "Dinner and dancing tonight?" I shook my head no, and he'd railed at me.

"You give us mixed messages," he said. "You laugh at our jokes, and then you complain about Will." I admit I did all of the above, but that didn't mean I had to say yes to him. Anyway, he was married. I could see that things were never going to improve for me in the shop.

I was the only woman to ever work in that shop environment, and worked hard to fit in. I'd laughed at dirty jokes while I learned to use heavy equipment. I ignored their sexist comments about women. I also went out with a man in the main building, not a good idea in the workplace. I saw my actions as fine. Who doesn't, especially at that age?

On the other hand, the men I worked with were public about their relationships, and they didn't hesitate to have relationships with co-workers in the main building. In any case, I shouldn't get whacked on the head and touched when I didn't give permission. Even Wally, the old groundskeeper, appeared behind me one day. When I was bending over to pick up garbage on the lawn, I felt a timid hand on my young blue-jeaned butt. Wally too? God.

"Are you going to quit?" my dad asked when I told him the story.

"Probably. I'm sick of nasty men. The guy with Polaroid photos of forty-one naked women in his desk. His little ear wax scoop thing. The guys are ranking the women with numbers. And I'm a seven, by the way. I might be an eight, but they'd have to see me naked to know for sure."

"Well," Dad said, "that's an all-male shop environment for you. I don't agree with it, but it's how it is. Maybe you can find a job with just woman. Oh, you'll have fun with that!" He was joking. I needed a college degree so I could get myself out of blue-collar work. Educated men wouldn't act like ogres, I thought. A degree could only improve my lot, and it was past time.

So, I went to college. I dreamed of college as a kid, but no one in my family went. Most people go right out of high school, but my life had been such a mess with my brother's death and my parents' hardships. At twenty-five, I flourished, my head deep in books. It was like when I was in grade school and sequestered myself in the attic, reading encyclopedias.

My senior year at University of Oregon, Ken came into my life. He wore a black motorcycle jacket and black-rimmed glasses and smelled faintly of some expensive cologne. His hair was pulled back in a ponytail. One ear was pierced in a row of tiny silver hoops. His whole appearance screamed, "rebel," and he'd worked at it. Despite thinking he looked pretentious and much too thin, I was attracted to him. I tried not to watch him, but I snuck looks during philosophy class. He had a way of looking irritated, but then softening to smile. His eyes were sapphire blue.

One day, he came in on crutches, and grimaced as he sat down. After class, we talked.

"Are you okay?" I asked.

"I'm not sure," he said. "I'll let you know in a few weeks. Little bike accident." His voice was low and smooth, as I'd imagined, but he seemed exhausted. Talking to him made my heart beat fast. A few weeks later, I returned from a long weekend. He noticed me trudging through Erb Memorial Union and said, "Looks like you had a great weekend." I hadn't. Two love interests made things impossible. I was also running back and forth between my two sets of parents.

"Everyone ended up mad at me," I said. "What did you do for weekend?"

He held up a crutch. "Not much. And I'm from Michigan so no family out here. I went to a friend's house, and we made dinner. It turned out pretty good!" He smiled. I liked this guy. That night at the computer lab, I kept an eye on him as he hobbled in and out of the lab to take sips on his Mountain Dew outside. After six hours of working, I said hi. It was close to 11:00 p.m., nearly time for the lab to close.

"How are you doing?" I asked.

"I got an essay done. Eight pages." He bounced his backpack on and reached for his crutches leaning on the wall. One fell, and I picked it up.

"You didn't need to do that," he said, "but I'm glad you did." He pivoted on his good leg, and looked toward the door.

"My car's outside. Can I give you a ride?"

"I'd appreciate that, to be honest." He smiled. We put his bike on the car rack with mine. He could hardly bear weight on the bad leg, but he somehow rode the bike. It was his only way to get to campus. Every night for two weeks, I dropped him off at his rental house. I worked to find parking close to the computer lab, to spare him having to walk on his bad leg. I looked for his gray bike everywhere. Then, he began leaving notes on my bicycle.

I started considering a relationship with him. Something real. He was getting better on his crutches and looked to be putting weight on. He needed it. I worked at Espresso Roma. We drank hot chocolate and talked every two hours when I had fifteen minutes. Ken said, "In India, people lie dying against the walls in train stations. You have to keep from stepping on them." It sounded exciting and frightening. I wanted to travel overseas, to see places far away. I'd developed a desire for adventure, and a "life's short, do it now" mentality since my brother's death. And Ken was a traveler, with stories to tell. Within a few weeks, we went from friendly to on fire for each other.

While we were writing the final for Philosophy class, I looked up to see Ken staring at me from across the writing table with those blue eyes. Then, he smiled his long, slow smile. His sweetness charmed me. Melted me, like butter in a hot pan. The two hours of writing were excruciating, a prolonged foreplay. We left the final and leaned against the cool brick building outside. We dropped our packs and kissed. The term was finished, and we'd have lots of time.

Ken told me he loved me first. It was New Year's, just past midnight. We were lying on a futon, housesitting for his friends. He kissed me awake to watch the New Year's ball dropping in Time Square on a color TV. I lay next to him, his arm around me. I loved his warm body. He was gaining weight and muscle, and looked better. He walked fine now, the leg healed.

"It's 1990." He went to the kitchen and pulled a bottle of champagne out of the fridge. "Want to go traveling with me this decade?"

"I'd love to," I said.

We clinked our glasses, and wrapped ourselves around each other. His long hair brushed my face like a silk curtain while we made love for the first time, the neighbor downstairs playing dulcimer music that drifted up. Later, we walked to the balcony. With the random firecracker still sounding around the university town of Eugene, he said, "I love you." I said it back. I thought, at that time, that we'd spend the rest of our lives together. It was a moment I remember clearly. I just knew. We shivered and looked at the night sky. Orion aimed his twinkling bow. We went inside and slept. From that day on, we were seldom apart.

I was at Ken's rental house sleeping, and woke up to someone pounding on the door. I opened it and an older guy in a frumpy suit stood there.

"Kenneth Cramer?"

I said, "He does live here, but he's not home now." The guy handed me a manila envelope.

"He's been served. Make sure he gets this envelope." If I hadn't been there, I wouldn't have known Ken was now legally divorced. I was relieved. We had talked about it a few months earlier.

"Hey, I should tell you, it doesn't mean anything, but I'm still legally married."

"Oh." I said. My heart sank.

"Well, my ex gets a big tax break for us staying married, and our marriage is just on paper. She has a boyfriend. It's just a financial agreement."

"Well, okay," I said, "But I won't live with you if you're married. You need to divorce her."

When the papers arrived, I was relieved, and I decided to stay out of it. His past was his past. It was wrong to pry in other's business, I thought. He was divorced now. That's all I needed to know.

By July, we lived together and he started graduate school in September. I managed a home for people with disabilities. I was glad to be earning money, and we had a small rental house. He talked about backpacker destinations, banana pancakes, and orange sunsets. My life was an open window, and I planned to fly far away with my love Ken.

4

$\mathcal{B}$aggage

Ken and I traveled around the Pacific Northwest and down the Baja Peninsula. We did road trips all over the USA. Those who love to travel know the serendipity of finding a good travel partner. Playing with time, rate, and distance was something we both enjoyed, measuring scale on the map with our fingers. It was the journey, not the destination. Ken drove the Subaru with his shirt off, drinking a Mountain Dew. I had bare feet, brown legs up on the dash. Truckers driving next to us honked and waved. We waved back.

Always, we discussed international travel. Ken told me of his travels with his girlfriend Sharol in Goa, India, where hippie women rode communal bicycles naked on the beach, the seats wedged up their butts. Ken wanted to explore Southeast Asia. After he finished his master's degree, we'd travel to celebrate. The last time he'd been overseas, it was in part to flee his marriage. A geographical relocation.

"I got married when I was only nineteen," Ken said. He looked down as he talked. "She played piano and read constantly. I'd known her since I was fourteen, and I left her for someone else while we were married. I was mean about it. She was always in my life, and I ruined it. I'm sure she hates me."

"I was a problem kid when she met me. I didn't even graduate from high school," he said. "She knew I was smart, and she believed in me. She started a business, and then, I rose to a management position at my job. We were yuppies, and we had a lot of money."

"So you rose in the ranks at work, and then left?"

"I just didn't want a traditional life. It was too soon. I had it all. Retirement and a gold watch was the only thing left, and I didn't want it that easy. I was wild as a kid, and I guess I got wild again."

"Well, we've all been young and dumb. Hormones hit some people worse," I said. I couldn't believe he'd been as bad as he described. I had seen glimpses of a bad temper, but nothing major.

He said, "I wasn't that young. I just wanted to travel."

"Why didn't you just travel on vacations?" I asked.

"I wanted to do rough travel, not two weeks in Hawaii. And I met Sharol," he said.

Sharol was a "looker," and Ken was her supervisor. He overheard her say she wanted a man with a tongue like a snake, and so their relationship was born. Leading a double life was stressful, he said. He bought two Valentine's gifts, kept odd hours, and when he wanted to leave the house, he pretended to be mad at his wife for being jealous. Then he stormed out and had sex with Sharol.

"I'll never live like that again," he said.

"Have you apologized?" I asked.

"I've made mistakes with her so many times, I'm sure she's sick of my apologies," he said.

Later, I talked with Dad. He said, "A leopard doesn't change its spots." Ken had been honest, though. It sounded miserable to deal with two relationships at once, but I could see his side. I had spent my twenties juggling relationships and ghosting people, although now I was ready to commit to a relationship with him.

He'd gotten married as a teenager, anyway. Too young. That was the problem, I thought. Who got married at nineteen, especially in the 70s? It didn't make sense. Maybe his family was conservative. I asked about them.

He said his mother, a lovely and kind woman, was the light of the family, but had issues with depression. Ken said. "When I was a little kid, she locked herself in the bathroom and said she was going to kill herself." This worried me. Did Ken have problems too? Ken said his dad reminded him to watch out for signs of mental illness.

"Do you think you inherited depression or something?" I asked.

"Sometimes I wonder," he said. "I make bad decisions and can't seem to avoid doing things that are bad for me. If someone suggests a course of action, I do the opposite. I question authority, even if it benefits me."

"Kind of like the bad choice is a magnet?"

He said, "That's how it was when I was a teenager. Girls and weed. I was always in trouble with school, my parents, sometimes the law."

I didn't want to think Ken was flawed in a way that would harm our relationship. I loved him. I hadn't seen the problems myself, so I could ignore them. He was self-aware, it seemed, and he told me everything. Maybe we weren't so different.

I wasn't married, so technically I hadn't cheated in my approach to relationships, a combination of polyamory and serial monogamy. I was a ghoster, disappearing when I was done with a relationship. Not a good thing, but it's the truth. I had some experiences so awkward I feel sick thinking about them. Once, an "old" boyfriend showed up at my Dad's house with flowers for me. The new boyfriend was there. I served them both lemonade and we sat awkwardly in the living room. I considered crawling out of the tiny bathroom window down the hall. I was young and inconsiderate. My parents had not been strong role models for relationships, so I blamed my bad habits on them. Now, Ken and I agreed to be faithful to each other, married or not. He said he'd never lead a double life again.

"Never again," he said. I had no reason to disbelieve him.

We were in love, sleeping so close together that I could hardly tell where my body stopped and his began. Spring arrived. We biked through Eugene and smelled the wild fennel. The roses bloomed on heart-shaped wires along the Willamette River bike path.

Despite my negative feelings about marriage, I changed my views. When he proposed, I said yes. I was glad that we were getting married, as I loved him deeply. And I wanted a baby—his baby. I talked with him about it in the springtime.

"No." Ken said. "Sharol wanted a family, and I wouldn't let her. Why would I turn around and have a baby with you if I wouldn't with her?" Absolutely not."

"I don't understand." I said. "You aren't with her anymore. We're in a relationship now. How does she factor in to our decisions?" I felt my heart pound in my chest. I felt anger flare, and swallowed it down. I wouldn't be angry with this man I loved. I wasn't very good at speaking up. Not at all. Oddly, I had no problem arguing with my parents, although Mom would slap me hard across the face with very little notice and no remorse at all. I had no problem arguing at school. In fact, I was on the speech team. With Ken, I didn't argue. Looking back on it, I was like a passive little rabbit hiding in the grass. In reality, I was a large, intelligent woman who should have been speaking her mind.

"I have no interest in becoming a drone," he ranted. "I'm not going to chain myself to this country to support a kid for the rest of my life." I stared at him. Never had I seen him so angry. He was shouting, frowning. I decided to wait to tell him that the pregnancy test had revealed two pink lines. Our birth control method had failed. That's all there was to that. I called Bell and her sister and told her what was going on. They lectured me nonstop.

"Don't listen to him. He's an ass."

"You can do whatever you want. He can't control you."

"Ditch him and keep your baby. He's not worth it."

And last, Bell said, "He's abusive and controlling. Can't you see it?"

I could see he was controlling, but I was tortured. I loved him. Was I wrong? Demanding? Ridiculous to think it was the right time to have a baby? I would do anything for Ken. Would he be there for me, for us? I fretted.

After a few days, I told him I was pregnant, and he was furious. His yelling overwhelmed me.

"It's not a baby. It's a zygote! I am not supporting this," he yelled. "It's not a good time. Later, we can have a family. Not now. I can't do this! You're only three weeks along!".

He followed me around the house yelling for three days, staring angrily and refusing to talk. I was miserable and cried constantly. Bell and her sister phoned and comforted me, insisting I didn't need to go through with his plan. But I did.

I take responsibility for the decision, but he put me under grave duress. I have kept this sad secret for years, all to myself. The regret follows me like a shadow, even now. After the abortion, I dealt with the grief silently and on my own, depressed and numb like I'd been throughout my teen years and early twenties. I guess I was willing to sacrifice everything for him, for love, for our relationship. It was such a mistake. When I was a young woman, I was too easily controlled by men I loved. That's the truth. It bothers me to put it in print, but I can't deny it. I was insecure, very much so.

I was attractive when I was thin, but there were times I wasn't. I wasn't obese, but just a bit too overweight to feel good in my skin. My friends argue that I was pretty, but prettiness came and went as my weight slid up and down. I was that chubby kid, and the pain of that never left me.

When I was a child, I lay in bed at night and fantasized about using a razor-sharp knife to carve fat off my body. First, it would be my stomach, and then my arms. My double chin bothered me too. I had started the habit of keeping my chin lifted up, so the beagle-like droop of my double chin wasn't so obvious. It didn't occur to me how horrible it was to think about slicing flesh off my own body. I just knew I hated being fat.

In an early photo of my siblings and me, I'm five years old, my brother four, and my sister nearly seven. He and I are chubby, with round knees and padded limbs. My sister is slender, with matchsticks for arms and legs. As a grown-up woman, it's obvious I was genetically inclined to be a large kid. I can now brush off the unfavorable comparisons with my petite sister, "Wow, you two look *nothing* alike!" I have something she doesn't.

I have FTO, the obesity gene, which I learned through genetic testing. Not that I needed the test. The pronouncements in DNA sites are often not that revealing, as in "you probably don't have a cleft chin," or "your hair is probably dark and curly." Mine was "you're likely to weigh more than average." No shit, Sherlock.

Some people say, "Why bother fighting your genetics? You do *you*," but huffing and puffing up stairs feels bad. So does struggling to bend over and tie my shoes. Aside from health reasons, others don't treat overweight people all that well—and I'm not morbidly obese, just a hair past overweight. A little obese. If you're a normal weight, think of yourself thirty pounds heavier. That's probably what obese is for you.

I've been dieting and exercising since I was a young kid. I still have a little booklet I made when I was nine, with a motto, WMLW!—We must lose weight!—and illustrations of *Sit-ups! Burpees! Touch your toes! Jumping Jacks!* Mom dated it and noted the year. She thought it was cute enough to keep. She had no idea of how miserable I was.

It all started in third grade. A boy told me he *had* been in love with me, but he said he was forced to move on to a skinnier girl. We were both eight at the time. Eight years old! I lay in bed that night fretting. Why was I fat? I pinched the flesh on my stomach, holding it aggressively between thumb and index finger. I was mortified.

I was nine when I realized that I weighed a lot more than most of my peers. When the nurse arrived to my fourth grade classroom with a scale, my heart raced. A quick solution—the lavatory pass! I needed to escape this humiliation.

When I came back from the lavatory ten minutes later, the nurse stared at me and gestured me to the front of the room. Dead man walking. I knew I was going to tip the scales at over seventy. Sure enough, I was a whopping seventy-two pounds.

Around me, other kids were shouting out weights. Petite Cheryl was fifty, athletic Kathy was fifty-eight, and *look who was well over seventy pounds*, more than some of the boys.

Truth be told, I wasn't the only one suffering on scale day. On the other end of the spectrum, little Thomas weighed forty-six pounds and after he was weighed, the boys swarmed him and carried him around the room, our teacher clucking like an angry hen. I went home unhappy. Maybe we had homemade macaroni and cheese for dinner. I ate slowly, and vowed not to eat seconds, which I probably did anyway.

By the time I was ten, I couldn't understand why my peers and skinny sibling—who ate the same food I did—weren't fat like me. Actually, why wasn't I skinny like them? It was a curse. In bed at night, I prayed to God—who I had little experience with—to make me thinner. Once, I pulled up the shirt of my little kid pajamas and saw that my stomach had sunk down into my ribcage, and thought he'd answered my prayer. I jumped up, delighted, and gravity returned my little potbelly. So much for divine intervention.

I didn't need God's help, really. I needed a nutritionist. My diet was a fat-and-carbohydrate smorgasbord of Cap'n Crunch, pizza, peanut butter and jelly sandwiches on white bread, and milk. Not only that, but I routinely sat in the attic with a single light bulb burning, reading my way through an encyclopedia set. I wasn't all that active.

My siblings and I ate like most kids of working parents. Some dinners were healthy, but plenty were frozen pizzas and Coke. And so it was that my brother and I, with similar genes, had fat little bellies, but my sister was as skinny as a toothpick. While it was partly a genetic issue, we were eating the wrong foods.

Other kids in my class were fascinated with my adipose tissue, and sometimes they groped me—intrusive assaults I never liked. Even the guy who leased twenty acres from my parents, a middle-aged man in plaid flannel shirt and work boots, grabbed my lower belly, pinching it hard and exclaiming "That's quite a spare tire ya got there, missy!" Why would an adult think that would be okay to do to a child?

Things got out of hand when I was about eleven. At that age, my body fat made it appear I had breasts. I don't think I had actual breast tissue, although maybe my buds came on early. The hard little knots girls get under nipples, like the antlers that a little buck sprouts, would have been a sure sign, but I don't remember them. I think I was just fat.

That was the year my classmates, led by a mouthy girl who later became a friend, clustered around me and advised that I *really* needed to wear a bra. *They* weren't wearing them, but I *really* needed to.

Finally tired of constant criticism, I talked with Mom and she bought me a "training" bra, the most uncomfortable thing I'd ever worn in my life. I'll never forget it. There were two little cushy soft panels that landed squarely over my chubby little breasts.

The satin straps, with no elastic at all, constantly fell down my shoulders. If I didn't wear the damn bra for one day, the judgmental girl gang would gather in a tight circle and gossip, shooting critical glances at my plump little-kid breasts. I was mortified, and if this was growing up, I wasn't enjoying it one bit.

Fortunately, I grew fast the summer between seventh and eighth, and was suddenly quite thin. That was the beginning of years of weight loss and gain. In my twenties, I didn't have a car, and walked about six blocks to get to work. The twenty-year-old me didn't arrive at work early, so I power-walked those six blocks. I was living on poverty wages (minimum wage), and I paid rent and electricity, so didn't have much for food. It was the poor person diet—no car, no money, no food. I got trim fast.

That changed when I got the job working for the State of Oregon, and I had money for rent *and* food. A year later, I walked into a local pub after a weight gain of twenty pounds—from thin to zaftig (Yiddish for "juicy"). My dinner was usually a corned beef and Swiss cheese sandwich from the corner market deli, supplemented with Coca Cola in a big cup with ice. Once more, my dietary choices weren't the best.

Stan, a dark-haired guy I knew from the local bar scene, walked up and said, "Oh, my God! You were the best-looking girl in this town! How much weight have you gained? Geez, turn around. I've got to see this."

This actually happened.

I remember looking at my friend Bell, whose jaw was to her chest. "Order to-go food," I told her. "I'm going to wait in the car." I sat in the cold car, rain rendering me invisible through the windshield. Bell came out with sandwiches after about fifteen minutes and comforted me,

"That asshole. As if he's any great shakes." I was miserable. When I went home, I ate dinner, then lay on my bed and dragged a blanket over my body and cried. Then, I got some ice cream, just like I did as a little unhappy fat kid. I tried to move on. Stan's insensitive remarks didn't motivate me to diet. At that point, I was in an eating phase. I'd return in my own time to frenetic aerobics classes, measured food in cups and spoons, and daily weigh-ins. I always come back to that eventually. Sometimes I just get sick of being the person who doesn't order dessert.

At twenty-five, I began community college full-time. That's when I began dieting again. I was surrounded by younger, thinner people, and wanted to fit in. Also, I fell in love with Matt, a guy who was blind. I was absolutely smitten with him. Matt was in student government with me, and his best friend sat in our student government office and described women for Matt.

"She's thin as a pencil, but has huge boobs,"

"Not bad, but about twenty pounds overweight."

"Perfect body."

"Oh my God, just *no*."

I knew Brian would tell Matt that I was not pencil-thin, nor did I have huge boobs or a perfect body. It made me anxious, so I took action.

I started dieting hard. This meant three PE classes per term, dance class, radical dieting, and then, bulimia. I can hardly admit it, but yes, bulimia. One night, I was in my apartment bathroom throwing up a dinner I'd eaten with Bell. Suddenly, I heard her voice, "What the hell? Are you okay?"

When I unlocked the bathroom door, she said, "What are you doing?" I'd reached a new low. Fortunately, I'd just started the bulimia, so I was able to stop. I just needed that voice of reason to say, "Too far. Enough."

That was just past the "Let's Get Physical" days of Olivia Newton John prancing around in leotards. I had a dancer's body and practically no body fat, and wore a size ten at 5'7". I felt mentally tortured, comparing myself to the women in the media. No matter how thin I was, it was never enough.

And the guy I had the crush on? It turns out Matt had a girlfriend already. He became a good friend to me, but he died of kidney failure due to his diabetes. His physical problems were much more devastating than mine, a strong reality check for me back then.

Back in the 90s, I was still that insecure fat girl, although then I was a tall, trim thirty-year-old girl with big green eyes and long brown hair. An insecure girl who terminated a pregnancy to keep a man. Him or the baby. She chose him.

I worked a lot and ignored my grief. I deserved to feel bad, I thought. I'd done it to myself. I'd let him control me, and with very little pushback. He seemed happy again, and seemed to think nothing of my silence. Now I realize he cultivated silent, unhappy women, like wilting roses in a dry garden. I've seen photos of his wife and his girlfriend Sharol, both with vacant eyes. I know that look. I saw it in the mirror every day. I wanted so badly for our relationship to work, but I neglected my own desires for his.

It became normal to feel sad again. It felt like an old pair of shoes. In time, we rented a small house. I managed a home for adults with disabilities. Ken went to grad school, and was closing in on his master's degree. He talked about school politics, but I was busy managing fourteen staff members and caring for the residents of the home. I was in my early thirties now. I tried to figure out my next career move. With my bachelor's degree in English, I didn't plan to manage a group home forever, but I didn't know what to do.

Around this time Ken decided we'd live in what's now called a developing country, never to return to the U.S. I found his plans scribbled on papers and in notebooks: "I can't wait to get out of this soul-sucking place," and "I've decided to completely quit academia." Even his New Year's resolution for 1990 was, "Third World, I'll be back ASAP!" He was a strong proponent of "need to know," and I guess he figured I didn't need to know, but his plans to leave our home in Oregon forever were obvious years later when I read his notes.

Back in my early 30s, I ignored red flags. As Dad said, "There ain't no 10s." I'd gotten so used to looking the other way when I was upset that I just carried on with Ken. If he said or did anything that concerned me, I took a deep breath and stopped thinking about it. This is denial in its purest form. Maybe ignoring his nasty behavior would reduce it. It seemed to help. I just walked out of the room when he railed about this or that.

I'd always told Dad I wouldn't marry a man who wore suits to work, as I thought the men in suits abused their power. What I conveniently overlooked was that before Ken's hippie days in Oregon, he'd worn suits to work. That should have been a red flag for me. I left that evidence aside, choosing to rationalize that he'd moved on from cheating with the office worker. He wasn't cheating on me. The truth is I thought he'd suffered some horrible childhood event that made him blow up sometimes.

Ken wore shoulder-length hair in a thin, curly ponytail, and by his mid-thirties was losing his hair, with a small circle of pink skin on top. In one ear, he had several piercings with silver hoops and onyx studs. He had a red beard and mustache, with a blond patch of hair under his lower lip. His eyes were sapphire blue, not baby blue like my brother's.

He was gentle with the people with disabilities at the group home. "Would you like some chocolate?" he'd say, and the five adults with disabilities gently encircled him with their wheelchairs. He had chocolate for all of them. He visited the people and they loved him for it. I loved him for it.

He loaded wheelchairs in the back of my red truck, and we went for rides and he took Mick fishing. Mick was a middle-aged man whose mom accidently backed over him when he was a little kid, causing him brain damage. Ken was so kind to him. He phoned me from next to the Willamette boat launch, "Deb, Mick's got to go to the bathroom! What do I do?" I coached him through handing Mick his urinal, in the wheelchair backpack. He called me three minutes later, "All's fine." He wasn't afraid of people who were different.

Yet, he could turn in an instant. Sometimes he got angry and said, "I don't like people." He had little patience for people who behaved badly. An intrusion on his privacy or a thoughtless act threw him into a quiet rage. He railed about his grievances to me, but he rarely said anything to the person who angered him. Most often, if someone made him mad, he simply disappeared. All communication stopped. His eyes went flat, and he held his lips together. Once, I told him I was mad at someone in my family. He said, "You don't need to get upset. Just do what I do. If family or friends want to control you or tell you you're wrong, just remove yourself. Go far away. Works great." He had a slightly angry expression on his face

"How do you think disappearing makes them feel?" I asked.

"It doesn't matter. They're the ones that caused it," he reasoned.

"But couldn't you talk?" I asked, persisting. "Maybe you could resolve the issue."

"I do resolve it," he said. "I leave. Let everyone think about it."

"Ken," I said, "That's not a solution. It's a punishment."

He shook his head. "You don't get it. There's nothing to solve.

People are judgmental and want you to change. Go away. Then, the next time they see you, they won't bring it up again."

"Is this about your parents?" I asked.

"It has been," he said. "But other people too."

"Your ex?" I asked him. I knew he carried some guilt over leaving his first wife for Sharol, who he partied with in hotel rooms while his wife worried at home.

"There was a lot that went on there. I was too young. We were successful. I felt trapped. I didn't want to do the house and the job and the pension plan yet." He looked at me. "With you, you want to travel, climb mountains. You're willing to. It works better for me."

While I liked adventures, I wanted the house and the family too. I wanted to carve pumpkins at Halloween, and celebrate birthdays. I was willing to give up some dreams at that point. We'd travel a while, I thought, and he was older now. He would want to settle down, wouldn't he? I was sure we would live in Oregon, near the mountains, the desert, and the ocean. Oregon was full of adventures, far away from his suburbs in Michigan.

Ken's plan to move overseas started coming together in 1993. That was also the year we got married. I'd been in no hurry to marry anyone. I'd learned too much about heartbreak from my parents. When I turned fourteen, Mom told me about her boyfriend, and later she made sure to tell me Dad had a girlfriend. It didn't take long before we were all miserable—all of us in the family.

So marriage? No. My parents' marriage had jaded me, and it seemed that my brother's death, my sister's jumping ship, and Mom's move into an apartment with yellow cigarette stains looping down the walls were evidence against the Great American Dream. We'd had it all—the farm, the piano, family dinners. Suddenly, it was a shambles. So, no way. I wasn't falling for it.

When I met Ken, my ideas about marriage changed. It was a love bomb, so much attention I was swimming in it. He said I was beautiful. He listened to me. He knew how I liked my coffee and read my moods. He watched me closely. I wasn't used to that kind of attention. I let down all the barriers and walls. I held nothing back.

41

We did everything together—college, meals, sleeping, travel. We got married on my family farm in June of 1993.

Our plan was to go to Bangkok as soon as Ken finished his graduate school exams. I was sad to pack up the wedding gifts we'd received only six months before, but we'd enjoy them the next year. Soon, we'd have a baby. Ken had agreed we'd begin a family when I was thirty-five.

"We'll be ready to settle down after our trip," he said. It didn't take a mathematician to realize we were leaving just before I'd turn thirty-five. I had my eye on a home and family, and maybe I'd begin grad school myself. As for Ken, he'd been working on his degree for nearly two years. It was time for the final capstone essays. He would receive a list of questions to choose from, and answer three in brief essays.

The master's degree exam should have been easy in comparison to his years of writing during university, but he was nervous. Sure enough, after writing the essays, he said he hadn't done well. After a team of professors graded his work, they asked him to rewrite some sections of the essays. He was quiet about it, then announced.

"I'm not going to be a professor after all."

"What?"

"I can't see myself getting a doctorate," he said. I knew he was now afraid to try again. He was miserable. He became quiet for days, moping around the house and not talking much. I was miserable too.

What happened here? He wrote incredibly complex essays while watching *Cheers* on his small black and white television, a joint burning in his Dirty Dick's ashtray, but he was giving up on the capstone essays? I was disappointed he threw up his hands so easily. He'd done the work, damn it. Get that degree. So what if he had to try, try again? The professors didn't want him to fail. Given his perfect grades at graduate school, it was unlikely he wouldn't pass on the second run.

I said very little, but I couldn't believe he gave up so easily. Ken sat at his computer. He put his hands together and held them near his chin, staring into space. Seeing him stressed was hard. It was hard to leave Ken with his thoughts, but I let him wrestle the demons without bothering him.

He was quiet for a few weeks after the master's degree exam, and then I think he decided, *fuck it, I'm done.* It was as though he'd dropped a tremendous burden. He seemed happier, and said we'd leave in January. We'd be gone six months. Maybe he'd finish his master's degree when we got back. I hoped so.

5

$\mathscr{B}$angkok and Beyond

Ken and I had one-way tickets to Bangkok. After that, we weren't sure. We discussed every country in Southeast Asia, but about Cambodia, I said a firm no. I'd seen black and white footage of the Khmer Rouge soldiers on television, and they'd killed millions of their own people by whacking them on the back of the neck or working them to death. Thinking back to how enchanted Ken was with Cambodia, I think he had his sights set on going there all along.

Our travels began in Thailand. When the fuselage door opened to Bangkok in January 1994, it was fifty Fahrenheit degrees hotter than Oregon. We got a taxi to Khao San Road, the traveler's mecca, found a place, and slept for six hours. We stood out as newcomers, as white as rice. People milled around looking at colorful hippie clothes and silver jewelry. They ate pineapple on sticks, or sat in open-air cafes and drank watermelon juice. We were hot and exhausted, but euphoric.

We went to a travel agency and booked transportation to an island far away, Koh Lipe. It was an edgy choice because it was a long ferry ride, and ferry rides in Southeast Asia are dodgy, as our Brit friends said. It took hours of buses, taxis, and *tuktuks* (four-banger carts) to get to the dock. Then, we took a long ferry ride across the Andaman Sea to arrive to Koh Lipe. I'll never forget pulling up slowly to the island. The aquamarine water was crystal-clear. We jumped in—it was up to our hips, although we had thought it was knee-deep. It felt like a warm tub. We got to the hot sand of the island and found a hut, a tiny thatched structure with dry palm leaves for walls.

Some backpackers told us that Thai-Chinese people occupied one side of the island, and the Chao Lai, Malaysian "sea gypsies," occupied the other. The competition for business could be fierce, and we were told the two groups hated each other.

In the afternoon, we went to a small restaurant to eat some green Thai curry, and a gecko landed on my head. Geckos drop their tails when they feel threatened, and the squirming, gelatinous tail wiggled in my hair, already a mess. As I jumped up to flip my head upside down to shake it out, the Thais and foreigners laughed. Someone said it was good luck. My heart pounded. I didn't like the gecko tail in my hair, but I didn't cry out.

After spending the night on the beach in our down-filled sleeping bags meant for the Pacific Northwest mountains, we woke up to a glowing pink and orange sky. Tiny hermit crabs scuttled around us. Next, a whale surfaced in front of the pink and orange sky. We heard the wheeze of water exiting the giant mammal, and saw a mist of water exit its blowhole. A school of dolphins leaped through the sea.

The sun got higher. Our western bodies, ten days removed from cold and rainy Oregon, weren't acclimated. Our long hair was filled with sand, salt water, and sweat. We desperately needed fresh water to rinse off. Picking up the sleeping bags, we trudged back to our hut, figured out where to shower, and packed our belongings.

We walked on a narrow trail through coconut trees and jungle foliage to the northern Sunset Beach side of the island, where it was quieter. The owner of the bungalow complex—four or five open-air beach houses made of wood—was a well-heeled Chinese woman, and she had small Lhasa Apso dogs that followed her around. She managed the open-air bungalows, made sure the workers kept the beach clean, and supervised the beach restaurant. We were a slightly more upscale group than the young backpackers of the loud-music side of the island. Just slightly. We were still a motley crew, wearing cotton clothes from India, smoking hand-rolled cigarettes, and drinking Sang Thip whiskey mixed with coke.

No accommodations were available when Ken and I arrived, but we met a German couple, Lindi and Ralf, who agreed to split the cost of a bungalow they'd rented for themselves and their two children. Lindi was petite, with dark brown hair cut in a bob. She was a calm woman and worried about her husband's temper. While Ralf was patient with his children, he tended to flare about small issues. He got mad if anyone used the communal bathroom without burning matches. Little things.

Each morning we were on Koh Lipe, Ralf got up at sunrise to do yoga. We watched his slim silhouette against the morning sky as he dipped down and raised his chest, arching up.

I liked the happy and playful sounds of children, and they constantly looked for shells, digging in the sand, and wading in a little pool we built for them with rocks. Ken liked Ralf's parenting style.

"That's how I want to be as a father," he said. Ken helped Ralf with the little ones, and Lindi and I drank coffee and watched the guys stroll the beach with the kids on their shoulders. I wanted to have a baby of my own, and felt sad watching them. We were older than Kati and Ralf, too. Regret followed me like a shadow.

During the days, we snorkeled, keeping a tally of the tropical fish. We ate vegetables and rice, and banana pancakes at the beach restaurant. Grad school was far away now. I hadn't seen him this happy for a long time.

After breakfast, Ken and I walked down the beach together. Sometimes we took the sarong, laid it on the sand, and slept. I'd wake up and watch him sleep, and he would wake up and stretch and blink his eyes. Then, we walked to the restaurant and sipped iced coffees and Coca-Colas, watching snorkelers emerge to call a friend over to see a certain fish. The sun set, and we watched it go down, orange and pink. At this point in our relationship, we had been married for about six months, but had lived together for four years. The future lay ahead like an untraveled road.

All the free time wasn't good. I wasn't used to having so much time to think. I struggled with seeing my brother's accident in my mind, the red car hitting the deep culvert, my brother spilling out, his friend screaming and blaring the horn for help. I worked for years to block that image. It's as familiar as my heartbeat, even now. Working a lot helped me not think about such things, but on the island, I wasn't working. Ken had his own ghosts.

On Koh Lipe, Ken visited the Buddhist Monastery. He met an English-speaking monk who showed him photos of a young deceased woman, stark naked. He showed Ken four photos of her body as it decomposed. Ken tried to look away, but the monk said, "Look, look." The monk discussed the fleeting nature of life, impermanence, and change as he tapped on each photo. The monk explained that photos of the girl's decomposing body also deterred the monks from ideas about sex. Given that the island was filled with young woman in swimsuits, I wondered how effective that was. The monk's photos bothered Ken because they reminded him of Sadie.

One night, he and his teenage friends left a party. Sadie and her friends were in a car just ahead. When Ken and the friends happened across her wrecked car and rushed to help, there was the metallic smell of blood, along with broken bodies and spinning tires. They waited for the paramedics to show up.

"It bothers me. I can't stop thinking about it," he said.

"It's because you're not busy with school or work," I said. "You have to stop thinking about it. Change the channel when you start." It was a technique I began to practice. Bad thought, change the mental channel. Think about history. Politics. The weather.

Keeping busy kept bad memories at bay. Our days on Koh Lipe were filled with snorkeling, relaxing in hammocks, and making sandcastles. We thought it was paradise until the first overnight experience at Sunset Beach. Ken and I got onto our mattress on the floor, with mosquito netting hung from the ceiling, and we wedged the net tightly underneath. We were glad to be sharing the bungalow with the German friends, and whispered for a while and kissed goodnight. We used some DEET before bed, and with the thick net, thought we were protecting ourselves from mosquitos. In fact, they weren't the problem. The problem was rats.

It was around 11 p.m. when we heard the squeaking. Silent and horrified, we watched them silhouetted against the night sky as their fat bodies poured in over the sills. We grabbed our flashlights and shone them around. They looked for food, soap, whatever they could find. As a person with a phobia of mice, this was terrifying. Ken comforted me, shushing me to let them forage, "Soon they'll leave," he said, putting his hand gently on the crown of my head. He was wrong.

The rats were in and out of the windows all night. I moved into the center of the full-sized mattress and lay on my stomach with a pounding heart. We tucked our mosquito netting as tightly under the mattress as we could. With horror, I shined my flashlight to see the rats, eyes glinting.

After that night, we approached the Chinese owner. Dressed impeccably in her pink flowered top and black trousers, she sat at a mahogany desk in a corner of the restaurant. Her small dogs nestled against her feet. When we suggested she use poison to eliminate the rats, she raised her eyebrows just a little, and said, "Let me think about that." While sipping our coffee, we realized that poisoning the rats might also mean poisoning her dogs. That explained why she wouldn't put out poison. As transient backpackers, we'd leave, and take our complaints with us.

We discussed a plan. We relinquished our space inside the bungalow to the rats, and set ourselves up outside on the large veranda, surrounding ourselves with seashells so we could hear the rats if they got too close. When we settled in that night, it was with a perimeter of a solid foot of seashells surrounding us.

This plan worked surprisingly well. That night, we heard them as they began crawling on the shells, and we kicked at them and hissed. Past midnight, I pointed my flashlight at some bananas we'd hung up from the rafters. A rat clung to it, rustling around and searching for a way in. I was so disgusted! We spent our nights on the veranda, while our friends slept in their bedroom, stuffing objects under the door to keep the rats out. They had children to protect.

It came time to leave the island, and we bought tickets on a day when the weather looked decent. Red sky at night, sailor's delight. While it was late February, the weather was bad, and overseas ferries are notoriously dangerous. This one was no exception. On the boat trip back to the Pak Bara pier, the sea was rough and the waves high. The people in the ferry sat below on benches and smeared Tiger Balm under their noses, throwing up in paper bags.

With the Thai passengers terrified, we tried to stay calm, but the situation was grim. We held hands a bit. We didn't talk much. Was this normal? No, it was not. I took Valium and Tylenol, my standard travel medications. The ferry was tossed around so vigorously that we didn't dare stand up. The one worker on the boat who spoke English sat down with us for a moment, grabbing the seat in front for balance as he fell into the chair next to Ken, visibly stressed.

"There is one life jacket on this boat," he said, "and it's mine." At this point, we felt we were in grave danger. Soon thereafter, we passed a fishing boat, just sitting in the sea and being tossed about by the waves. The Asians below deck with us talked excitedly. A Thai boatman threw a heavy coil of rope, and workers on both boats worked back and forth to connect. Now we were towing the fishing vessel. The young worker came below and explained the situation. Apparently, the fishermen's motor had malfunctioned, and they'd hoped for the ferry to appear. Had it not, the boat would have gone down, and the men most certainly would have drowned. The water seemed a bit calmer, or maybe we were distracted. The sun came through the clouds.

Knowing we helped the fishermen in their boat cheered us up and distracted us, and we watched as the small boat was towed along. When we reached the dock, we realized with despair that getting off the boat would be dangerous. We had to disembark during the "sweet spot" when the sea lifted us up to the height of the dock, but not much higher. The boat was either depressed below the swells, or held high aloft. Many people had to be forcibly yanked off the boat, as they were afraid to make the jump. Men on the boat would hold a crying and terrified woman, and then shove her across into waiting arms. I procrastinated stepping forward, as I was afraid.

Ken made the leap first, then turned and looked at me. I was terrified. He stood on the dock watching me, broadening his stance and mouthed, "Now!" every time we hit the sweet spot. He had agreed to catch me. He stood on the dock, water dripping from his face. He looked at me, frowning and with his head down so he could see me above his glasses. We locked eyes. The dock went up and down a few times before I jumped. When I did, he grabbed me so hard he lifted me off the ground. My heart pounded hard. We had survived the ferry.

Looking back on our adventures now, I shake my head at some of our hard travel. I'm not a stranger to discomfort and poverty. I learned early on I could tolerate anything for a short amount of time. Ten years earlier, when I'd started college at twenty-five, I was dirt poor. Because I was in my mid twenties, I wouldn't dream of taking money from my parents. I'd been earning my way for a long time. I was an older college student. I learned to live hand to mouth—to squeeze ketchup into a cup, add water, and heat it up for soup. My first few years of college, Dad helped me pay for tuition in exchange for taking care of my stepmom. She had seizures, and he traveled for work. It was a fair trade and helped me get started in school.

My second year of college was harder. I rented a room in a miserable house in Lake Oswego house with Bell and Jonathon. Jonathon used a wheelchair due to a skiing accident. He had the bottom of the house, and I had a room on the second floor. Jonathon terrorized me, wheeling around fast on my heels and yelling. He smoked joints, and turned his music up to the loudest possible volume, trying to annoy me as I studied.

I asked Bell, "What the hell is his problem?" and she said she used to sleep with him, but not anymore. He blamed me for his inability to get her into bed. She and I had rooms upstairs, and I was more fun than him at that point. He was smoking too much pot and angry all the time. I reminded him of his sister, who he hated. Great. When Jonathon moved out, mad that he hadn't chased me away, we were stuck with a huge rent and we couldn't afford electricity.

Now we lived in poverty. I could have moved back home, but Bell had this dog and cat she wouldn't desert. It's hard to find housing with pets, so I stayed and threw in money until she could find a place. We gathered and burned scrap wood from a nearby housing development project to keep warm, and slept on the floor by the woodstove. One night, Bell's cat chased a mouse over my body. We lived for two months without electricity, using daylight and candles, and cooking with a camping stove. It was mind over matter. I kept my grades up and paid my bills. Then I transferred to University of Oregon.

I lived in poverty my third year of school, too. Back then, people thought if you went to college, you had money. No. I was surviving on loans, term to term. They didn't cover food, rent, or bills. I worked as much as I could to cover expenses, but cheap housing was the only way I could survive.

I rented a room near university in one of those huge, old houses with a covered porch. My room, with wooden floors and a five-foot tall window, looked out onto West 5th Street with broadleaf maple trees. The owner was Hal, who claimed he was related to one of Hollywood's richest families. He seemed wealthy. He had a one-man sauna constructed around his toilet, with a hole on top for his head to poke out. Food in, food out. He was experimenting with not showering for a full year, with unsurprising results.

Desperate for a place to live, I rented a room in his large house. He populated it with street people, a "social experiment." I wanted to move, but finding a place was hard during a term, especially with Oregon rain and family issues. My grandma died on the thirtieth of December, and I was shattered.

It took every ounce of willpower to get through that trimester. I didn't want to end up back in blue-collar work with guys putting pornography and snakes in my desk. I had to get my degree and get a decent job. I knuckled down and ignored the lunacy in the house as best I could. The skinny forty-five-year-old who threw furniture around the house at night, and the hangers-on with red scabs on their faces were always awake, smoking cigarettes outside. I didn't know them, and I didn't want to.

One night, a gentle, young woman meandered downstairs naked looking for food. I was studying at the kitchen table. Melissa explained in a soft voice that she was with a guy living in an upstairs room, and she previously lived at a women's shelter. I handed her a blanket from the back of the couch in the living room.

"Isn't it all fascinating?" the landlord Hal said about the random people who just showed up at the house. His oversize tweed jacket enclosed his personal atmosphere, barely.

The heating was powered by a giant basement furnace, into which we shoveled barrels of wood chips. Stanley, the wiry guy who threw furniture around at night, said "Don't worry, friends. I've got this." He was gracious, and it took effort to keep the furnace going. When the wood chips ran out in early February, Oregon's coldest month, it was like living in a Charles Dickens novel. I stayed in my small room with the wooden floor and tall drafty window. I had plenty of studying to do, so it wasn't all bad. Turning on lamps helped heat my room. I pointed the gooseneck lamp onto my pillow to warm it before I got into bed. We housemates started talking. Stanley said they thought I was a rich bitch at first. I was the only one paying the full rent of $200.00 per month. That was a week's worth of pay from the old accountant I worked for on weekends and after classes.

"But now we like you okay," he said.

The drafty old home's hot water was plentiful and we took turns with long, hot showers. Then, the water heater broke. We turned on the stove for heat and drank tea. The coil burners glowed red in the dark kitchen at night, and I slipped downstairs at night to turn them off, or someone else did.

By the end of my third year of college, I knew how to live poor and deal with it. If I had just one room, I could make it mine, even a small space for just a bed and a desk or table. I dealt with rough travel in the same way.

For now, the adventures in rat-infested island huts were fine. I could tolerate the discomfort, especially for the beauty of the tropics and because I was with Ken. Soon enough, we'd book return flights. We'd live in Michigan or Oregon. Ken would finish his master's degree, and be a teacher. We'd have a baby and a home of our own.

After the ferry ride back from Koh Lipe, we returned to Bangkok and stayed near Soi 4. We'd check out some nightlife before our next travel adventure. Our first night in a bar included an encounter with aggressive bouncers. As soon as we got seated along the back wall of a nightclub, the bouncers locked the door, stepped in front of it, and blocked foreigners—men and women alike—from leaving. They wanted more money. We watched foreigners blocked from exiting after paying their tab and arguing with the woman at the cash box.

It's hard to say no when a tiny woman looks at you and says, "You buy me lady drink?" but we knew better. Lady drinks were ridiculously expensive, and while the girls drank water, the barman tallied up a drink bill, padded with additional fees. A small bowl of peanuts, 200 baht. Wet towelettes, 200 baht. We watched the door for a while, opening graciously to admit guests but slamming inhospitably after unpleasant arguments over the bill. Time after time, we watched as foreigners grudgingly took out wallets and anted up more money. We decided we weren't doing that.

When we tried to leave, the bouncers locked the doors, trapping us. We refused to pay the hugely inflated bar tab, and stood our ground, although we'd seen them kick one guy in the backside already. When Europeans and Americans started to enter, we called out, "Don't come in here! They don't let you out unless you pay triple the price!" After several people turned around and went elsewhere, the bouncers let us out. They were happy to see us leave, and we didn't get kicked in the backside, either.

One evening, we were at one of the Thai bars watching kickboxing and drinking. It was refreshing to see something different than the usual Thai bar scene entertainment. Things were a lot different in the early nineties. Thai dancers might paint each other to look like butterflies with pink fluorescent chalk and perform under black lights, which seemed innocent enough. Once, we walked into a bar to see tiny dancers squatting on stage to eject toads into tall glass containers. Who came up with these ideas? Bangkok in the '90s was often just plain seedy.

We found a Thai Kickboxing bar with lots of westerners. Between kickboxing acts, a guy went on stage with a big sack. We didn't know at first that his squirming and heavy white-cloth bag held snakes, and when he opened the sack and used a long stick with a hook to pull out his first snake, Ken's eyes lit up and he sat up straighter in his seat, "Ooh, snakes!"

For as long as I'd known him, five years at that time, Ken had a fascination with reptiles. As a boy in Michigan growing up with two younger brothers, there was a snake incident in which a long garter snake crawled into the aluminum handlebars of a bicycle. Their poor mother had to deal with it, positioning a garden hose with running water to "motivate" the snake out of the handlebars. Ken was excited with this snake handler and the squirming bag full of tricks. Not me.

I was glad to be a safe distance from the stage. The snake handler called volunteers onto the stage, and one scantily clad young Western woman got on stage to "help." A snake placed around her neck by the handler took the short journey down underneath the front of her flippy little top, and raised its head, revealing her bare breasts. She was embarrassed, and the snake handler quickly removed the reptile, while the audience roared with laughter. It could not have been choreographed.

Many snakes later, the handler pulled out his final offering—a green snake. The audience fell quiet. Did they know something we didn't? Could this be the infamous two-step snake of Southeast Asia, a snake so venomous that its victims fell after the second step? Ken slammed down his drink and headed for the stage. I watched him, stunned. We always looked out for each other, and I didn't like the looks of this.

"Not this snake," the handler seemed to be saying, shaking his head. Ken was not to be turned away. He was on the stage now, and he was determined to handle the snake.

"Okay, hold the head like this." I saw the handler speak slowly and deliberately to Ken, making sure to stare Ken in the eyes. This guy knew how to handle a lit-up western man.

Ken took the reptile from the handler. He looked straight at me and smiled widely. Next, he did a little dance around the stage, gliding the snake expertly through the air. As quickly as he'd made his way to the stage, Ken carefully handed the green snake back to the handler, and got off the stage. He returned to his seat laughing as audience members, stunned at his audacity, applauded enthusiastically. Some even sent him drinks. I was quite impressed, and we laughed about it the next day, when we were both sober.

"Did you know that was a venomous snake?" I asked Ken.

"Well, yes, but they should all be treated like venomous snakes."

"Were you having fun?"

"Very much so! I love snakes. You hold them right behind the head, control them. They can't go anywhere if you hold them right."

I can't deny that I didn't enjoy living on the edge. And our adventures were high adrenaline most of the time. So many opportunities existed in Southeast Asia to get in trouble. I learned that later.

6

Vietnam

At the Lao Bao border crossing into Vietnam, Vietnamese guards at the border beat poor people back away from us. One woman was desperate and begging, pointing at black teeth in her mouth. Ken and I were very upset, and wanted to get through so the guards would stop hitting and kicking at the people. We said very little to each other. When we got through the crossing, we gave away all the medical supplies we could part with—all the aspirin and pain relievers we had. Then we moved down a dirt road. Vietnamese people walked by us on different trails, with huge baskets of fruit, cases of coca cola, and vegetables. It was late in the day now. We came across a row of huts, a brothel. Young women in pajamas wandered around, and border guards sat at tables outside drinking tea. We rented a hut with bamboo cane walls. It had a hard dirt floor. We lay our sleeping bags on cots, and used our padlocks to secure the door.

I watched the Vietnam War of the 60s and 70s on television as a kid. Sometimes we made Dad turn the TV off so we could eat dinner without the war blasting around us. My parents talked very little about the war. Pro war people were the squares, the conservative men in suit and tie, and the women who didn't believe in women's lib. They were the "establishment" of the country. Status quo.

The war protesters were dissidents and hippies, in tie-dye shirts and often smoking pot. When they were on TV, Dad said, "I guess we're squares," and Mom said, "I guess we are," and then Mom turned off the little black and white TV and we had dinner.

I became aware of hippie culture when I was nine or ten. I remember peace signs, the yellow happy face buttons, "Yellow

Submarine" bumper stickers, bra burning, and all the smoking pot going on everywhere but my hometown Canby. My grandmother lived in a house on the family farm, and I asked her everything.

"Gram, what's 'the pill'?"

"Darling, women use it to prevent having babies."

"Why don't they want to have babies?"

"Dear, after three or four, women get awfully tired."

"Oh. But babies are so nice."

"Some women want to do different things, darling."

"Like what?"

"Jobs, darling. Careers," Gram said. She took a drag of her cigarette. She'd had three babies, and lost one when she fell on hard ice. She'd also attended University of Washington and was the smartest person I knew.

"Oh," I said. "Which is better, babies or a career?"

"Most women have to choose. It's hard to do both. Maybe ask your mom," Gram said. Fat chance there. Mom always said, "Wait 'til you're older."

Talks with Gram gave me a lot to consider. Men had children and jobs. Why couldn't women have both? I pondered that. Mom usually came home from work and did all the laundry and cooking.

Dad came home and worked outside, then ate dinner. Then, she'd supervise us kids doing the dishes. She worked constantly. Dad made more money, though. Maybe that was why she worked more at home. It didn't seem fair to me. Every day, I went to Gram's house after school until Mom was home from work.

Grandma was my trusted source. If she didn't want to tell me something, it must be really juicy. I could usually fill in gaps with magazines lying around her house. Gram saw me reading the *Reader's Digest* story about Charles Manson's followers murdering Sharon Tate in California, a horrific event in the U.S. in the 1960s.

"Do you think you should be reading that?" she asked.

"It's pretty gory," I conceded. I couldn't tear myself away. Grandma never stopped me from reading anything.

"The Manson cult took things too far. They were on LSD,"

Gram said. I experienced my first cognitive dissonance in thinking about the Manson cult. Charles Manson and his followers were hippies, who were supposed to be gentle. Yet, they'd murdered people, which was anything but. It was the 60s. Nothing was black and white, except for the television.

Was it wrong to protest the war? Yes, but no. Dad said, "It doesn't matter whether or not you support a war, you have to support the troops." And that was that.

My parents weren't interested in talking about politics, but they didn't need to. I grew up immersed in the cultural revolution of the 60s and 70s. President John F. Kennedy was assassinated when I was five years old. I remember it. I was in grade school when Martin Luther King, jr. was assassinated. I remember it. We all knew his brilliant "I Have a Dream" speech. Gloria Steinem and feminism gave us girls some ideas, too. Why couldn't we wear pants to school?

When I was twelve, girls were permitted to wear pants after we had a "sit in," a peaceful demonstration near the principal's office. Previously, we had to wear dresses, every single day. *Ebony*, a magazine about African Americans, showed up in my high school library. I had friends who wore bracelets engraved with a U.S. soldier's name on them, a soldier missing in action or a prisoner of war. In eighth grade, our social studies teacher Mrs. Dwiggins taught us about Watergate, which was going on at the time. I was steeped in politics and 60s culture, surrounded by it, raised with it.

Year after year of my childhood included some cultural event that gave me pause. The Ohio National Guard shot some university students at Kent State, Ohio in May of 1970. They were protesting U.S. bombing in Cambodia, a country bordering Vietnam to the west. All of these events came back to me as I traveled in Southeast Asia. When I began traveling, I was thirty-four, and remembered Vietnam from memories that went back to my very early years growing up on a farm.

When I crossed into Vietnam, I noticed the people worked hard there, constantly moving. Silk dresses were made at tailor ships, and in towns, women and men pushed little carts of food around. The women balanced carrying sticks with heavy loads of vegetables in baskets.

The history of the Vietnam War was never far away. One Vietnamese double-amputee in Saigon told me, "Madame, here we call it the American war." Traveling through the countryside of Vietnam, giant shell cartridges propped up sides of grass huts. Souvenir shops sold knock-off Zippo lighters with U.S. army mottos and engraved names of soldiers. We took it all in, Ken and I. We were so lit up with excitement we could hardly sleep, looking forward to seeing places we'd only experienced in books and on television. I felt more alive in Vietnam than I'd ever felt.

The My Lai Massacre site, where U.S. soldiers killed a village of men, women, and children, had been turned into a tourist exhibit. I knew about My Lai. I studied it when I was in a summer history class at University of Oregon in 1989. Ken knew about it too.

In March of 1968, an American military-led massacre of a village full of old men, women, and children occurred at a place called My Lai. American soldiers killed some 350 or so civilians. We went to see it. At My Lai, giant white statues depict Vietnamese people in protest and grief. One statue is of a person raising her fist in the air—a gesture of power and solidarity. Another statue of a woman holds one arm straight up, while her head and other arm loll to one side, as if her mental strength continues while her physical body fades.

When Ken and I arrived, I began to cry. Tears streamed down my face. The air at My Lai buzzed with cicadas. Otherwise it was silent. Two Vietnamese gentlemen approached us and wanted to shake our hands and pose for a photograph, which we were supposed to take with our camera. They seemed to appreciate my tears, so they asked me for some cigarettes, or money. This cheered us up, and Ken and I smirked at each other. Opportunists were everywhere in Southeast Asia. We usually saw them coming.

Ken and I gave them cigarettes and a few dollars. We entered the museum and walked around. Some photos were barbaric. Black and white images showed Vietnamese people being pushed from the open doors of American helicopters high in the air, with the person circled to make it easy to see. Ken murmured he'd been told this hadn't happened, but the photographs seemed real.

Helicopter photographs hung on the wall, with small typed captions that helicopters kept coming, helicopters kept coming. Each photo depicted the helicopters getting closer. You could almost hear the blades of the helicopters.

I thought of the Life Flight helicopter in the 80s, landing outside of the hospital where Dad lay in the ICU—the percussive chop of helicopter blades, and people wailing as they streamed into the tiny waiting room where I sat. I fled, getting out as fast as I could, holding my breath. The horror of the helicopters at My Lai brought back the helicopters at the hospital, where Dad was struggling to live.

When U.S. airplanes were bombing Vietnam during the war, Vietnamese people dug tunnels and lived underground. We went to check out the Cu Chi Tunnels with Lucy, who we'd met in Nha Trang, a beach town in Vietnam. Lucy was in her late twenties. She bargained aggressively and traveled well. She was generous with her sesame crackers. We were glad to take in some extra carbohydrates, as we were getting downright thin, especially Ken. Children followed Lucy, as her long, blond hair attracted them. She ended up traveling with us, and we shared meals or stood around uncomfortably as she bargained for her cookies and rice crackers, whittling off perhaps a dime.

Some of the Cu Chi Tunnels were enlarged for Western tourists. We passed through them easily. Above the underground stove were a number of small holes venting the kitchen fire, so there wasn't one large billow of smoke—which would have been seen and bombed by U.S. planes. The dirt in the tunnels was packed hard, and the tunnels were well organized. After that tour, the Vietnamese guide asked if we wanted to travel underground in an actual tunnel that had not been enlarged. Of course! We got into the tunnel about ten feet, and it was tight. We crouched down and waddled like penguins, hunched over tightly. I backed out when I saw spiders the size of my hand.

I walked along above Ken and Lucy, and listened for their voices. When they emerged about 200 feet from where they began, they sucked in air, and were soaked with sweat. Lucy got stuck trying to squeeze her hips out of the exit hole We pulled her out. Ken's gray cotton shirt clung wetly to him, and his hair was soaked. The guide walked us to a watering tank for livestock, and Lucy and Ken splashed off.

We were getting closer to Cambodia, and Ken wanted to go.

"Those women we ate dinner with said it's really interesting, and security is good," Ken said.

"I don't care. It's the one place, the one place I didn't want to go. Look, I'm not interested. I'm afraid of it there. The politics are crap! Didn't you hear what the Khmer Rouge did to some prisoners? They fried people's livers on a spit and ate them!" I knew too much about Cambodian politics. I kept talking.

"It's been several months of hard travel, come on. Look at us." I stared at him. We'd both lost about twenty pounds. I looked haggard. He looked skeletal.

Ken listened.

I continued, "We're already here in Vietnam, a country we were at war with just a few decades earlier, and it's been kind of intense. We've been in ordinance fields, we've crawled through the Cu Chi Tunnels where you nearly collapsed. I don't mind hard travel, but no. Let's go back to Thailand."

Ken nodded. "I guess we could skip it, but it would be interesting. I'd like to see that torture museum and the 'Killing Fields'." In Phnom Penh, the places of torture and murder had been made into museums. Oh, boy.

"Ken, look. I understood the importance of remembering such things, but torture museums shouldn't be the main draw, should they?"

"Angkor Wat's there too! It's on par with Machu Pichu and the Coliseum in Rome," Ken said.

"Let's just go back to Bangkok, and we'll go to Nepal, or maybe

India? I haven't seen the Taj Mahal."

Ken shook his head, "No, it's okay. Maybe we'll just go to North Vietnam, see Hanoi." He looked disappointed, and looked down. I hated letting him down, but why couldn't he defer to me?

"Do you really want to go?" I asked him. He brightened, and said, "Yes, I really do want to go."

"Okay, then. One condition: if I don't like it, we leave. Promise?"

"Sure." He leaned in and hugged me. "But we're only going to be there for a few weeks."

7

Cambodia

Our first day in Cambodia, was August 19th, 1994. I was struck at the openness of Eastern Cambodia. It was a hazy sky, fairly clear, but the sky was not a saturated blue. Palm trees and rice paddies were all that was to be seen, except for the occasional beggar sitting on the ground lifting prayer-folded hands as we drove by.

Ken really wanted to be in Cambodia, and I was apprehensive, but here we were. We were still traveling with Lucy. We caught a taxi on the Cambodian side, after crossing border control. We rode in the backseat for hours, and then the taxi driver stopped five miles east of Phnom Penh and said, "Okay. Here we are. Phnom Penh. You want me take you some hotel, some place, extra five dollar each pax. Up to you." He actually said "pax." It's a travel word that means person, an abbreviation that's not meant to be said.

Lucy said, "You take us to guesthouse in Phnom Penh, or we give you five dollar LESS each pax. We NO give you money if you no take us to city. Up to you!"

He looked at her, with brown eyes.

She looked back, without blinking. Green eyes, master bargainer. Clearly, he'd met his match.

He said, "Okay. I take you."

The three of us in the backseat avoided commentary the driver might understand, but we had plenty to say once we were dropped off at Capitol Guesthouse in Phnom Penh. We couldn't have imagined that particular ploy to get more money. Another few months in Cambodia, and we could have.

We spent one night at Capitol Guesthouse for next to nothing. Young and middle-aged men brought prostitutes to the hotel at all hours, slamming doors, arguing the price, dropping glasses and bottles, and singing and laughing. The Capitol was a sweaty stage for nasty habits of men visiting Cambodia. I was the only western woman staying there, I noticed. I spent the night trying to ignore men yelling, "show us your tits!" and singing drinking songs. I was disgusted when my flashlight rolled under the bed with the dust and used condoms.

We were older than most travelers on a shoestring, and The Capitol with its two-dollar meal, complete with gritty cooked greens swimming in garlic, was not enticing.

Lucy didn't like Phnom Penh. She said it was like science fiction, an apocalyptic and dismal place. We thought Vietnam was light years ahead of Cambodia with decent electricity. The Vietnamese people worked hard, and didn't seem to be in a state of collective grief.

After visiting the temples in Siem Reap, she left, freaked out by the recent Khmer Rouge kidnappings and murders on Route 4 that everyone in Phnom Penh was talking about. It's one thing to travel in a developing country, and quite another to travel in one with murders to westerners occurring.

An Australian, a Brit, and a Frenchman decided to travel to Sihanoukville riding on top of the train. That sounds like the beginning of a joke, but it was no joke. Not at all. The embassies had warned that the Khmer Rouge soldiers were active on Route 4 and they were hijacking the train between Phnom Penh and Kampot too.

The train ride looked interesting. People rode on top, fun for adventurous backpackers. The train snaked through the southern part of the country before stopping at the beach community of Kampot, or Sihanoukville. We all talked about such adventures, those of us who backpacked around SE Asia in the '90s. I imagined the three young men debating whether or not to take the train:

What are the chances of anything happening?
They probably won't do anything to us. We're foreigners!
Embassies always make the warnings stricter than they need to.
Awww, fuck it! Let's just go.

This was all conjecture. On July 26th, just after 2:00 in the afternoon, Khmer Rouge bandits attacked the train. When the Australian, Frenchman, and Brit were discovered, the Khmer Rouge kidnappers took them to Phnom Voar.

The owner of Capitol Guesthouse told people the young men asked him about the price difference between a taxi and a train to the beach. The difference was a few dollars more expensive for a taxi. Not that a car would have been safer. Khmer Rouge attacked national Highway Route 4 back then, and recently, three young restaurant workers had also been pulled over on Route 4, marched off and killed.

All of us in Phnom Penh talked about the three kidnapped men. We hoped they'd be released. Many of us talked in the bars about their decision to ride on the train. Sure, it was a poor decision, but hadn't we all made risky choices? Ken and I had toured Vietnam fields with unexploded ordnance lying around. We were young, and believed that it had been detonated. Who knows what was a foot underground, though?

According to newspapers, the men were made to work in the hot sun. Two were already ill. At that time, kidnappings could earn some serious money, but eventually Cambodian middlemen got things all mucked up. The mountain was bombed by the Cambodian government, and the Khmer Rouge killed the three young men. This was the situation playing out when we arrived in Phnom Penh, and it was in the press every day.

Ken and I left Capitol Guesthouse and stayed at Lotus, a guesthouse owned by two Singaporean men—a large-bellied man with dark skin in a white turban, and a short, gregarious man who said he'd been a pastor. He'd left a huge congregation and a wife to flee with his girlfriend.

Downstairs was an ice-cream parlor, unique in that day. To have ice cream was special, and we happily paid $3 per scoop for it. Strips of rubber hung between the dining area and the kitchen, and air conditioning in the dining area felt better than the heat and humidity outside and in the kitchen, where the pregnant Cambodian wife of the larger man cooked the food. She also did all of the laundry. In fact, she worked from sunrise to sunset.

On my 35th birthday in September of 1994, Ken bought me a huge bowl of three scoops of different kinds of ice cream, including delicious Rum Raisin. It was served with candles on it. The owners sang to me, and Ken and I shared it with two spoons. Later, I took advantage of my birthday status to talk about baby plans, a topic he wasn't ready to discuss.

"Ken, women can't wait as long."

"You're healthy. I think you'll be just fine."

"Even if we get pregnant right now, I'll be nearly thirty-six," I said.

"Let's do this later," Ken said. And that was that.

While the downstairs ice cream restaurant was clean and cheerful, the upstairs guesthouse was anything but that. It had thin walls and padlocks to use on the plywood doors. One day, I went to stand on the balcony and watch the crazy traffic in front of P'sar Thmei. As I walked back to my plywood cubicle, the Nigerian in a room near ours reached out and grabbed me by the forearm, hissing, "Come here! Come here *now!*" as he dragged me into the room. I resisted, and pulled my arm away with all of my strength. I shouted, "Let go!" His hard penis showed through light cotton pajamas. My heart pounded in my chest, and I yanked my arm away. His fingernails scraped me. I scooted away and down the hall to our cubicle.

Red half-moon fingernail marks showed where he grabbed me, and ribbons of blood trailed down my arm. I locked the door, and got out rubbing alcohol pads to clean my arm. When Ken came back, I told him the story. He walked to the Nigerian man's cubby and knocked lightly on the door. The man answered.

"Did you touch my wife?" Ken asked. I heard the mad voice, his icy tone.

"I'm sorry. I didn't know, sir," said the man.

"Don't do it again," Ken said, and the man closed his door. Apparently, the man thought I was a prostitute. Why else would a white woman be in a ramshackle hotel in Phnom Penh?

"We're leaving tomorrow morning," Ken said. We did, too. We stayed at a hotel near the Foreign Correspondent's Club of Cambodia. Everyone called it the FCC.

A few days after the Nigerian guy tried to pull me into his plywood bedroom, a military policeman stopped the cyclo (bicycle cart) I was in. He made me get out, had me turn around, looked me over, and then motioned to sit on his motorcycle. Now I was being treated like a "taxi girl," which was the Cambodian term for prostitutes. Taxi girls were everywhere, mostly tiny Vietnamese women in short skirts and skimpy tops.

When we first arrived, Phnom Penh was a strange dystopia with its messy electric wires crisscrossing from the electric poles and the monsoon floods around Central Market when it rained. The rats swam around in flooded streets, and in my first week there, I was riding a cyclo and one swam next to me. I hoped it wouldn't get in. I saw a boy aiming a slingshot. I looked up to see what he was aiming for. When I looked down again, he was spreading the black wings of a dead bat. He looked me in the eyes and smiled. I smiled back.

8

$\mathcal{K}$hmer Rouge

The Khmer Rouge (Communist Party of Kampuchea—the SPK) killed up to two million of its own Cambodian people from 1975 through 1979. The mass genocide is considered one of the worst crimes of the twentieth century, all the stranger because it was Cambodians killing Cambodians. Around the time that South Vietnam fell to the Viet Cong, the dirt-poor Khmer Rouge soldiers marched and drove tanks into Phnom Penh and took over. They destroyed banks, burned money, and abolished religion in Cambodia. Anything western was dismantled.

Khmer Rouge soldiers evacuated the wealthier Cambodian people from Phnom Penh, killing government workers, people who spoke French or English (the languages of capitalist western culture) or any other languages except for Khmer, those who wore glasses (a sign of an education), and Khmers of mixed heritage (they wanted a pure race). They killed the weak as they limped along. Anyone who couldn't march out was shot.

Led ideologically by Pol Pot, the Khmer Rouge wanted Cambodia to return to an agrarian society. They forced the Phnom Penh residents, some who had never done manual labor, to work rice crops in the sweltering heat from sun up to sun down. The city dwellers learned to hide their identities: those with glasses buried them. Those with government-issued identification got rid of it fast. Government workers were shot. Anyone who had previously held power of any sort was murdered. People learned to play dumb, to shut up and be silent.

The Khmer Rouge soldiers worked the city people hard, and they died of illness or exhaustion. They tortured and murdered Cambodians who they suspected of any wrongdoing.

The Khmer Rouge were still active in Cambodia when we arrived there in 1994. We didn't think they were a threat to us. They were in the northern part of the country, and launched a dry season offensive each year. The head of the Khmer Rouge part, Pol Pot, was alive and leading his party when we arrived to Phnom Penh in 1994.

Khmer Rouge bandits were engaging in kidnapping and murdering people on Route 4, the highway that ran from Phnom Penh southwest to Sihanoukville. It was closer to us.

In 1994, I exercised in a Phnom Penh gym and looked down to the pool. I peddled on an exercise bike, imagining the government workers who were lined up and shot dead, falling into that same pool. I think the pool was drained when people fell into it, shot dead. Maybe it's the memory of my imagination.

Tuol Sleng S-21 Torture Museum had hundreds of black and white photographs of Khmer Rouge victims, and those victims included a couple of young American men—long-haired, sad-eyed guys from the U.S. who were sailing around off the coast of Sihanoukville.

Rumor had it the guys were waiting on a shipment of Thai stick to deliver back to the U.S., and had sailed around the coast of Thailand for weeks, passing time. When their sailboat was spotted near Sihanoukville, where Ken and I later lived, the Khmer Rouge rushed out in speedboats, boarded the sailboat with machine guns, and then delivered the young men to Tuol Sleng S-21 Facility. They were interrogated and tortured, just like everyone else.

Tuol Sleng S-21 was originally a high school, but the Khmer Rouge made it into a torture facility in 1976. They arrested and imprisoned their fellow Cambodians, and interviewed and photographed them. They interrogated, tortured, and then killed them. The prisoners slept on the ground and were shackled. They were fed tiny amounts of gruel, and were often forced to drink urine and eat feces. The torture facility has been maintained so that visitors can witness the atrocities endured by the prisoners. It's now a Genocide Museum.

We were nervous about going. Cambodia already seemed pretty bleak, with bumpy dirt roads and electric wires looped from pole to pool. We rode up on motodops, who waited outside for us. Once inside, the tragedy unfolded in a collection of photographs. Black and white photos of the victims, posed with numbers pinned to their prison garb, cover walls and walls. Terrified images of people stared at us as we walked through. In one photo, a woman sat in a mechanical-looking chair. A long thin metallic device in the back of it was adjusted to touch the back of her head. A tear ran down her face, or did I imagine it?

Some people had broken noses and bloody lips, staring up with dark wide eyes. Some of them smiled, posing for the camera. Many photos were young women with messy hair chopped short, Chinese revolution style. Many photographs showed emaciated people. Even a couple of Westerners were pictured. Worst of all were the pictures of young children, with their innocent eyes. There were even babies.

All of the people in the photos were tortured and murdered by interrogators, who accused the victims of crimes against the Khmer Rouge regime. The accused were brought here blindfolded, then sat down and photographed as soon as the *krama*—the ubiquitous checked scarf—was taken from their eyes. The photos are devastating to view.

The photographs in Tuol Sleng S-21 Genocide Museum were horrific. They were more disturbing than the shackles attached to beds and walls with heavy chains. They were worse than the oil paintings of prisoners being water-boarded, or shocked with electricity, or carried with wrists and ankles tied to a long plank, like livestock being taken to market.

The photos, all the same size, were worse than the map of skulls that used to be displayed at Tuol Sleng. The sheer volume of the photographs was disturbing beyond measure. So many people were tortured and murdered.

When Ken and I went in 1994, the museum was silent, and said to be haunted. We were overwhelmed by the photographs, and looked closely at many of them. In one room was a large photograph of a man shackled to a bedframe, bloated and misshapen. He'd been tortured.

Ken and I had only our thoughts as we walked through Tuol

Sleng Genocide Museum. We wandered like ghosts through the museum. Because we worked as teachers, knowing Tuol Sleng was a school before it was a torture and interrogation center added a layer of horror. It had been fifteen years since the Khmer Rouge had been driven out of Phnom Penh in 1979. That was the year my brother died. I thought back to my brother's funeral. 1979 seemed like just a few years before.

It had not been long since the Khmer Rouge were torturing people here. Not that long at all. I also realized that as with my brother, there was nothing here that could help anyone interpret the events. I lacked a guide. I could have used one. The Cambodians could have used some counseling, too. The entire nation of people was experiencing collective grief, for a third of the population lost. It must be such a heavy burden.

9

$\mathscr{L}$iving the Dream

Despite its horrific history—and some of it in the making--Ken and I wanted to stay in Cambodia. So many different people lived there, the Cambodians of course, but people from all over Asia, too. People from all corners of the globe worked in NGOs—non-governmental organizations. Médecins Sans Frontières, The Red Cross, American Friends Service Committee, Cambodian Mine Action Centre, Hope International, and many additional agencies existed to help the Cambodians recover from years of horror. They'd been bombed by the U.S., killed by the Khmer Rouge, and occupied by the Vietnamese (who, to be fair, fought the Khmer Rouge and rid Phnom Penh of that bloody regime). It was an international mix of people doing important work with the Cambodian people. The country was full of opportunities for people who wanted to help the Cambodians. I was that person. So was Ken.

The sensory overload of Phnom Penh made me feel alive. Crossing streets was an adrenalin rush with motorcycles swarming in front and behind us. Women wore checked kramas on their heads on which they carried giant fried spiders and locusts to markets. Jewelry cases held rows of gemstones, many of them genuine rubies and sapphires from Pailin. Silver elephants, silver birds, and even silver purses hung from market stalls outside. Brilliant purple orchids and orange bird of paradise flowers lined the front of Central Market. We were in a place so different, and the Cambodian kids loved to chat.

"Hello, mister and madam! Excuse me. Are you Ahn-glay?"

"No," I'd say, smiling.

"Oh-strah-lee?" the kids asked.

"One more guess!" I said.

"Amerique!" and then, the children laughed and smiled.

We decided to teach English in Cambodia. We'd planned to teach before we'd even left the U.S., and this was the place. The

Khmer people were hungry for education, and English speakers approached us everywhere we went.

"How old are you?"

"How many children do you have?"

"Do you have sisters and brothers?"

"How long have you been married?"

"Do you like Cambodia?"

It was tiring, I can't lie. Ken and I had the patience, and didn't mind most of the time.

We dug the wrinkled photocopies of our university degrees out of the bottom of our backpacks, and bought work clothes at P'sar Thmei—the central market. There were piles and piles of clothes for sale, probably donated by American churches. Ken had some white shirts sewn up quickly, using his wedding shirt as the pattern. He got some slacks made at one of the tailors on Sihanouk Boulevard. Bolts and bolts of light wool fabric were pulled from shelves so Ken could pick what he liked.

We got hired at the American School the day we applied. The owner was a Khmer American woman who glanced at my fake ruby ring, and said "I only like white stones," meaning diamonds. She was covered with gold and diamond jewelry. Ian, an Australian, taught there. Jill, a young British woman, taught there too. We now had some friends.

I taught a kindergarten class, and had a young Cambodian assistant teacher who could speak some English. I taught the children English-language songs, and the little five-year-olds sang "I'm a Little Teapot," and shouted out colors. What drove me away from teaching at the American School was the class of older boys. I was lost with them.

I'd ask the boys to sit down, and they'd yell back, "Sit down, sit down!" I'd say, "Stop" when they were jumping from desk to desk, and they'd yell back, "Stop! Stop!" Ken was experiencing similar issues, and when we heard about the Australian Centre for Education (ACE), we decided to apply to teach there. We weren't used to ten-year-olds running us over.

At ACE, they were paying good money—$22.00 per hour, I think—and teachers taught five different classes per week. Each class was an hour and a half, and met three times per week. Class time with students was twenty-two and a half hours, and it was assumed we were prepping for several hours. After teaching children at the American School, neither Ken nor I wanted to teach the children's program. With my degree in English Literature, I planned to teach adults. Ken's degree in philosophy qualified him to do the same. Having photocopies of the diplomas was helpful.

We went to ACE, interviewed with the director, and were hired on the spot. I remember telling my students at the American School I was leaving. I had one adult class there, and my students were disappointed. Reasey, one of my best students, wrote me a poem about the moon. Another woman gave me a silver bracelet. I was sad to leave, but the pay was double at ACE.

I liked going places with cyclos, which are carts with wheels, men sitting high above and riding their passengers through the streets. The cyclos were slow, so I started using the motorcycle taxis, called motodops.

When I started riding motorcycles in Phnom Penh, it was with motodops. The drivers, clustered outside restaurants and gestured, running to their motorcycles with one hand up high, saying "Madame! You go with me? Moto?" The first time I went with one, I put my leg over the saddle to sit astride, kind of awkward as I was wearing a skirt at the time, and several men whistled and laughed, shouting, *"Oooooy,"* the equivalent of catcalls. Ken said, "You're supposed to sit sidesaddle, like the other women do." It seemed dangerous to me, but soon enough I rode sidesaddle.

My new friends at ACE school were Malgosia and Lelani. We used to stand at the back of the school and smoke cigarettes and talk. Lelani was from Greece. When Lelani's long skirt got sucked into the back spokes of a motorcycle on the riverfront of Phnom Penh, it tore the skirt off her body, and sent her flying onto the asphalt. I took note and was careful to gather my skirt and tuck it under my body when I rode with motodops.

At ACE school we stood around with other teachers, sharing news we'd heard about the three western guys who Khmer Rouge kidnapped off the train heading south to the beaches. Most of the time, Ken and I avoided the gossip and grieving over the three kidnapped men and also of three young people killed on Route 4 by Khmer Rouge. The three young adults were driving in a taxi to Phnom Penh to get supplies for their restaurant at the beach, named Rendezvous, when they got stuck in a convoy hold-up. Khmer Rouge soldiers abducted and shot all three of them.

All over Phnom Penh, westerners and Khmers alike talked about the killings, and many knew the young couple. Even people who didn't know them suddenly developed relationships and cried about their deaths. This was 1994--the year we moved to Cambodia. We both had our own losses we'd worked through, and it didn't make sense to grieve people we didn't know. Ken didn't want to leave. If we didn't talk about the deaths, we could carry on and live here. That didn't stop us from following the news closely.

At least now the young foreigners in the community realized the Khmer Rouge warnings were no joke. The embassies sometimes politicized information, but their warnings were heeded. As time passed, things quieted. We settled into teaching and normal daily activities.

In those early days, Ken and I were on adrenaline every minute, avoiding being run over crossing the street to reach Central Market, or struggling to order food, or hearing some amazing tale of adventure, or seeing flocks of dog bats at the temples up north. The drug of constant adventure in a beautiful tropical place is addictive.

Ken and I got settled in to Phnom Penh. Our first apartment was along the riverfront and just south of Independence Monument. We watched traffic on Sothearos Boulevard from our first floor apartment, just up from ground floor. Nearly immediately, we had two motodops who were there when we went outside—smiling men who didn't speak English but understood us when we said ACE or P'sar Thmei or other places we went. They sat outside our apartment and it soon became clear that they weren't going anywhere. We'd acquired our own personal motodops.

We were learning the ropes around the capital. P'sar Thmei translates "Market New," but in English language it's called Central Market. It's French colonial yellow, and built like a huge dome, with spider-like tracts running out in four sections. Back then, between each of the legs of the market were smaller markets covered with tarps. Now it's much fancier. Central Market used to be a huge draw for us, but we had a lot to learn.

The beggars overwhelmed me. The first lesson was that giving money upon arrival to the market ensured we'd be swamped with them. Getting too friendly or engaging beggars meant the amputees followed us and rubbed their limbs on our arms to get attention. We kept eyes down and walked fast. Money belts were tucked deep into our pants, and spending money was deep in a front pocket.

"You have to be mean when we arrive," said Ken. "Give money on the way out."

"I'm not good at being mean," I said.

"I know," he said. "Just do what I do."

We kept our eyes down all the way in to the market. On the way out of the market, we distributed *riels*, the Cambodian currency. Then we crossed the street. The traffic circle around P'sar Thmei was a constant stream of motorcycles, so the heavy traffic created a barrier between the beggars and us. We let the motorcycles weave around us as we held hands tightly and waded through shoulder to shoulder.

Another lesson we learned was to distrust groups of busy children. At P'sar Thmei were groups of children who surrounded foreigners and pickpocketed them. They chattered and laughed with a tourist, first touching the foreigner's arm hair, and then worked at confusing and throwing him off, encircling him. Then, they'd get into pockets and the wallet was gone.

It wasn't just kids trying to make a quick buck. When we arrived in 1994, just a year after UNTAC had scooted out of Cambodia, the

Cambodian people in Phnom Penh were trying to find sources of income. Moneychangers figured out that they could easily shortchange most foreigners. They were on corners around the market, sitting outside with small glass-windowed money carts. They shortchanged us often, but we caught it and got indignant, pointing at the exchange rate written on the glass stall window. The mistakes were obvious. They'd sigh and give us the extra money.

After the market, we occasionally went to La Paillote for an icy Coke. Charlie, the owner, was Swiss and married to a Thai Woman. La Paillote was a popular place during the UNTAC era, and it remained a good restaurant until Charlie's death.

La Paillote was our favorite restaurant after we got settled down in Phnom Penh and could afford meals out. The Thai waiter would bring a basket of homemade bread nestled in crisp white napkins, along with icy butter. French bread off the street was full of bugs from the Khmers baking at night, but there weren't bugs in this bread. We ate the same thing every time, Fish Florentine and chocolate cake. It was across from P'sar Thmei, so when we went outside to get on our motodops, we gave money to beggars. We often found ourselves arguing with other westerners.

"Don't give money to them. There are agencies for that," they'd say. Ken and I said nothing. It was useless to argue. Poor was poor, and people needed food. We bought them food sometimes, too. Later on, adults began using the children to beg for them. Buying food seemed the better decision then.

After eating, we might head home to hang out in the apartment. We wrote letters and postcards. E mail and social media didn't exist then. We headed to Phnom Penh 3 Post Office to unlock a little mailbox and pick up letters. We routinely had mail from our parents, friends, and Ken's brothers. At home, we opened letters excitedly. We lay on our bed, with the overhead fan on high and read letters aloud, rereading the parts we liked and talking about news from home in the U.S.

At night, we went to The Heart of Darkness, where Ken and I were friends with the owner, Samnang. It was before The Heart turned into a disco club. It had a bar, some tables, and one pool table in a back room with a short corner. We spent lots of time at the riverfront, too. The huge Tonle Sap Riverfront in Phnom Penh was lined with tall apartments and restaurant buildings, porches overflowing with bougainvillea flowers. The length of the river has a long promenade. It was an easy place to pass time. The westerners sat in the restaurants and watched the river. Cambodian people walked the riverfront, jogged at sunrise and sunset, and spent time sitting on the benches and eating snacks. I bought wishing birds from an old lady who packed around a square wire cage.

I always purchased a bird, held it in loose hands, made a wish, and released it into the sky. The old lady laughed and nodded her head. Ken smiled too.

10

Teacher, Teacher

At ACE school in Phnom Penh, Ken and I taught five classes each. We taught about twenty-two hours per week, and prepped for eighteen hours. Other teachers shared lesson plans with us, and in time we reciprocated.

I had western and English-speaking friends from all over the world. They were transient, leaving after a year or two, but new friends arrived. One day, Andrew, a teacher in his mid-forties, fainted rather unexpectedly. A lot of us struggled with that on occasion, as having stomach problems for days and becoming dehydrated set the stage for blacking out. Andrew went to Bangkok to get things sorted. When he returned, he'd had a brain surgery.

He said, "A worm traveled through my bloodstream, and set up base camp between my skull and the brain. It laid eggs, which hatched." We were horrified. Brain worms? He'd gotten the worm from eating greens that weren't washed well enough. Around that same time, a young British teacher died. He had hepatitis for some years while traveling and couldn't stop getting drunk every night. I remember one of the coordinators at the school crying in her office, the wailing floating outside.

Cambodia attracted a lot of druggies. People overdosed on opiates, or had accidents because of drinking or other drugs. Khmer newspapers splattered death scene photos all over the front pages, the overdosed young adult sprawled on a bed, or hauled out of a lake, or fallen from four stories on the cement below. Ken and I resolved to stay out of the newspapers.

One day, a provincial manager, Sebastian, breezed into the top floor of the school. He wore a blue and white-checked krama from the provinces around his neck. He smiled widely, and his white teeth shone out of a tan face. His blue eyes and golden-blond hair made him look like a poster child for Europe. He was from Holland, and spoke Khmer and English well.

The teachers swarmed around him in the upstairs lounge area at ACE, and excitement buzzed around. As the provincial manager for the Sihanoukville Branch and with the danger that existed around Route 4, we were in awe. We stood around with other teachers, and asked questions about teaching in Sihanoukville. As it turns out, he was looking for staff. He smiled at Ken and me.

"A couple would be perfect down there."

Sebastian said the pay was good, the freedom in the provinces was better than Phnom Penh, and the coast was beautiful. Sihanoukville sounded better by the minute, except for the Khmer Rouge. We'd just started teaching at ACE Phnom Penh, and I wasn't ready to leave. Ken would persuade me soon enough. He was good at that.

The Phnom Penh ACE building, a huge building with perhaps a hundred classrooms, had old tile floors and dark bathrooms, the toilets splashed with urine. Some classrooms were cool, with old air-conditioning machines that dripped fluid and got a frosty appearance. Some rooms were downright insufferable, with air conditioning that didn't work at all. ACE was at the north end of town, past Wat Phnom and near a roundabout that led out of the city, to the Boeung Kek Lake. The money was good there, but the provinces sounded more exciting to everyone.

There was an ACE branch in Siem Reap, home to the world-famous Angkor Wat Temple Complex. Siem Reap was like heaven to Ken and me. It had beautiful old buildings, quiet streets, and the nearby temples. Walking the long promenade to get to Angkor Wat, with the large carved stones underfoot and small children jumping into the waters of the moat to either side, is an experience. The vast size of the temple, which has several levels, is breathtaking.

Its carved walls reveal ancient legends entirely foreign to most western eyes, and even before I understood the history and religion of Cambodia, I appreciated the beauty of the bas reliefs at Angkor Wat. Ken and I went to the temples so many times, and often had them to ourselves. It was quiet in the provinces.

Sihanoukville was a quiet beach community, with a few nightclubs and rows of palm trees along the road coming in. The air was clean and fresh, particularly in the morning and after a rain. During the monsoon season, rain fell so hard that that it was deafening. The palm trees outside our windows would shake under the rains. Sokha Beach was most popular beach back then, and there was an open-air restaurant that served pepper crab, fried squid stuffed with sausage, fish sprinkled with coarse salt and pepper, and papaya, banana, and pineapple. A local seal would cross the road just up from Sokha Beach. Sihanoukville belonged firmly to the Cambodian residents. It was a sleepy beach town.

Hearing about the provinces gave us wanderlust. Ken and I decided that the provincial teachers had an interesting gig. Away from the critical eyes of administrators in Phnom Penh, young teachers ran the schools, and led adventurous lives. Ken talked with me before he put his hand up for us. He was eager to be one of the provincial staff. Anyplace remote, edgy, and dangerous was his realm. I was attracted to the idea of living at the coast, but concerned about the Khmer Rouge.

"The danger," said Ken, "is not in Sihanoukville. The danger is in *getting* there." He was right. The area between the capital city and the beach town was not safe, with Khmer Rouge hijacking trains and pulling over cars up and down Route 4.

"Ken, if we go, how long do you want to stay?" I was looking to the future. "I don't want to commit."

"Let's get down there and see what it's like. We'll fly. We aren't getting on Route 4."

"Okay, then. Let's do it." We agreed to put our hats in the ring to teach at the provincial school in Sihanoukville. This decision changed the course of our lives.

We had a lot to talk about before we moved to Sihanoukville. Route 4 had gobbled up six westerners. Days before the fateful train ride of the three young men being held captive at Phnom Voar, the bodies of the other three young people had been recovered from Route 4, the young couple with a restaurant named Rendezvous in Sihanoukville. I avoided thinking about the six westerners, but their deaths brought up issues for me. I could rarely hear about a death without thinking about my brother.

You could say I had complicated grief. It was all mixed up with my parents' relationship, and while I reasoned with myself that no one was to blame for his car accident, I couldn't help thinking it was our fault he died. We let him down.

Before Warren died, Mom and Dad had a trial separation. They played tug-of-war with him, which was hard. Then they got back together after Mom's year in an apartment. My siblings and I resigned ourselves to more family drama. We'd been through more than enough ugly relationship drama at home. Snappy responses. Uncomfortable silences. Harsh words and car engines starting up. I moved back to the farm when Mom went back. Dad had begged and begged her to come home.

My brother was sick of the drama, and he went to live in North Portland with his friend Tim, whose tiny house smelled like fried potatoes and engine grease. When brother came back to spend a hundred-degree day in Canby, he and a buddy partied all day at the river. At 2 a.m., drowsy from food at the local truck stop, my brother drove off the road and hit a deep culvert by Top O' Hill restaurant, a few miles from home. It immediately stopped his car, which went end over end.

His friend survived, and crawled back to the upside-down Chevy Malibu and honked the horn, screaming for help. My brother lay on a small strip of lawn soaking the dry summer grass with his blood.

Fifteen years later in Phnom Penh, neither of us knew the six westerners in Cambodia who had died—three while driving on National Route 4 to get restaurant groceries, and three while riding on the train heading to the beach. Ken knew I was bothered, though. Just the thought of death was upsetting. With complicated grief—chronic grief all mixed up with other issues-- sensory images triggered me. A song by Steve Miller, the smell of strawberries, a hot day in June. The color blue. All these made me think of my brother. Memories made me stop everything and grieve. See images I couldn't shake. Dream. Ken knew it, and tried to keep me from worrying.

"It doesn't make sense to grieve for people we don't know," said Ken. He didn't want me to think about the deaths of the westerners. If I did, I might just want to leave. Everyone in Phnom Penh worried about the deaths for various reasons. Would the money flowing to Cambodia dry up? Would tourists be afraid to enter the country? And what about the families of those killed? They must be so upset. Of course they were. Devastated.

We signed contracts for three months, which stipulated that we wouldn't travel on Route 4, owing to Khmer Rouge murders of the six young foreigners. We could fly back and forth from Phnom Penh to Sihanoukville, hopscotching over Khmer Rouge bandits on Route 4. Phnom Penh was quite literally the big smoke, which is the Australian nickname for a city. Exhaust from motorcycles filled the air. Women cooked with huge woks and soup kettles set up on food carts, with wood burning to heat the wok. The bars were full of people smoking, with ganga and tobacco in the air. Even years later, Pol Pot went up in smoke with old black tires burning underneath him.

Our plan was to fly to Sihanoukville when the new term started. Now, we had a few months more in Phnom Penh. We did our own shopping and cooking and cleaning, although the landlady constantly asked if she could clean for us. We could have used the help, but we felt funny hiring a maid. I'd worked as a maid during college but I couldn't wrap my head around having one. I washed all of our clothes myself and hung them outside over the railing on our balcony. The sun was so hot that wet clothes dried within an hour. One day, as I sat in the living room, I saw a long stick poke up outside and snag one Ken's t shirts. When I jumped up and ran to the balcony, the thief ran down the street. I learned to be more careful fast.

11

*U*ndone by UNTAC

UNTAC was the United Nations Transitional Authority in Cambodia. Essentially, the United Nations decided that Cambodians needed help, so they formed UNTAC and ran the country for a few years. Cambodia needed democracy and elections, so UNTAC ran an election in which Prince Ranariddh won. Hun Sen had been prime minister until that election, and he refused to step down.

Bert's Books was a place where the UNTAC people clustered to swap stories. Bert was a good source of information, and had a great sense of humor. With a law degree, he'd spent the UNTAC years stationed up in Siem Reap, talking "rule of law" to Cambodians with an interpreter at his side. Bert sold T-shirts that said, "Always Carry a Book…You Don't Look So Dam' Stupid," and Ken bought one. We learned our first lessons about UNTAC from Bert.

Some claimed the UNTAC election unfairly pitted Hun Sen against royalty, and the Cambodians love their royal family. In any case, when Prince Ranariddh won the UNTAC election, Hun Sen didn't accept the result. Finally, it was agreed that the two would share the prime minister position. Of course, power-sharing in a country run by the "spoils system" doesn't work. A main benefactor needs to exist, the father at the top showering underlings with favors. That benefactor gives favors and jobs to his followers, and so on down the line.

In Cambodia, the trickle-down flow of money has been referred to by one long-term westerner in Cambodian as "corruption on steroids." Most Cambodian people I've talked to say, "That's just how it is."

UNTAC brought boys, boys, boys to town, and they wanted girls, girls, girls. A result of UNTAC'S presence in Cambodia includes the boost in sex-trade workers—from 6,000 to 20,000 in Cambodia in 1992 and 1993. This led to the crisis of AIDS in Cambodia. A friend of mine in Cambodia told me that Hun Sen was asked what UNTAC's legacy to Cambodia would be. In one word, he answered "AIDS." It wasn't talked about much, but it was in everyone's minds with all the taxi girls and sex trade in Phnom Penh.

Steve was a friend in Phnom Penh, good looking with dark shiny hair and blue eyes. He could be charming and funny, but his reputation wasn't great. He was a salesman, just kind of a fast-talker. He said, "Deb, I'd hit on you if you weren't married." And I said, "Thanks, Steve." He loved women. Maybe some of the men disliked him because he was good-looking, but he was self-absorbed too. He'd talk his way into a job, then show himself to be a lazy employee.

He spent a lot of time with taxi girls. Ken and I saw him around town ridiculously drunk, sometimes passed out on an old vinyl couch in someone's bar. When his British girlfriend and I went out for drinks, she was quiet but on her third glass of wine, she told me he was HIV positive. She worried he'd infected her, but she got a test, then six months went by and she got another. She was lucky. The tests were negative for the virus. Steve tried to continue sleeping with taxi girls but well-placed rumors in Phnom Penh and Sihanoukville stopped girls from sleeping with him.

Ken said, "Of course I'm going to warn them. He's out throwing money around and getting drunk. How many girls has he infected?" He needed to be stopped. He eventually left the city, in part because the taxi girls in Sihanoukville and Phnom Penh were giving him a wide berth. His work reputation was bad, and now, no more sex.

In the 90s, the taxi girls in Cambodia weren't like European sex workers who monitored their health. Prostitutes, mostly Vietnamese women in the 90s, were afraid to get checked, or said they couldn't afford to. They were very poor. Men paid additional money to skip using a condom.

Another UNTAC mistake was that UNTAC disarmed the army members who *fought* the Khmer Rouge, but not the Khmer Rouge themselves, which lends credibility to the bumper sticker, "When guns are outlawed, only outlaws will have guns." So, the renegade Khmer Rouge still had their guns. Every year, Ken and I read about the "dry season offensive" in the *Cambodia Daily*, with the Khmer Rouge army fighting up north with the government army.

UNTAC was a big explosion of international money to support imposed democracy, sex, and foreigners in Land Cruisers with big per diems and Cambodian workers who were paid well. UNTAC was finished in 1993. It left behind Cambodians without the inflated salaries, it left behind a government with two leaders (two heads are not better than one in Cambodia), and it left behind Land Cruisers and memorabilia, with those highest on the pecking order looting the goods. Sex workers remained, looking for the next boyfriend. And yes, UNTAC left AIDS in its wake.

No one I've ever talked to thinks that UNTAC worked, but it was a golden ticket for some of the Khmer people. Many of them made their life fortunes during UNTAC.

12

$\mathcal{S}$ihanoukville by the Sea

In January 1995 we flew to Sihanoukville, named for King Norodom Sihanouk, to teach English for ACE. The old Russian aircraft had round windows that fogged up, and the pilot was a round-faced Khmer. The Russian co-pilot kept a fifth of vodka nearby. I only know this because on subsequent flights, the crackerjack Khmer pilot invited me to sit on a jump seat behind him and the co-pilot. I was afraid of flying, and he knew it. He laughed and said, "Don't worry, little sister! I don't want to die either!" The Russian co-pilot, with his pale skin, blue eyes and red-veined nose said nothing, but seemed to be watching the flight.

On this occasion, I didn't yet know the pilot. I sat in my seat, heart pounding. When we approached the airport, the flight attendant told us to fasten seatbelts. I prayed silently. Looking out into the dry field, a windsock was hanging from a pole. Then, I saw the water buffalos. At least six of them were milling around the airstrip. As the plane got closer, I noticed that others around me were murmuring and commenting. I clutched the armrest tightly and it came off in my grip. In the nick of time, the buffaloes scattered, running this way and that. My heart was in my throat. We had landed! Ken and I squeezed hands, relieved.

Sebastian, the Dutch branch manager, met us at the airport. He was happy to have some friends in Sihanoukville, and we had lots of dinners and conversations over the next ten weeks. He'd recently disagreed with the director of the school, and we listened to his complaints. We could see his side, which had to do with contracted jobs outside of the school.

At ACE Sihanoukville, we taught for the regular English program at the school, but the administrators in Phnom Penh also sold contract jobs and we travelled to other businesses near Sihanoukville and taught classes. One job entailed traveling to the beer factory, Cambrew, a drive out near Route 4, to teach English. Another job meant traveling a road with jungle and lots of brush to teach at Ream Navel Base.

At Ream, the plan was to teach the Cambodian Navy how to speak English to communicate with the Australian military who trained them in technical matters. Sebastian's gripe, and later, Ken's, was that the long drives were out of town. We weren't supposed to leave the safe confines of Sihanoukville, but when the Australian government and the school administrator wanted us to, it was safe.

The drive to Ream Naval Base was especially worrisome. The road meandered along a brushy area near a hilly region. It narrowed in places. Ken taught for a term at Ream, and I taught at Ream the next term. I was recovering from food poisoning or giardia, so I felt ill all the time. On top of that, I felt anxious about my personal safety. I was driven there by a Khmer bodyguard decked out in a green military uniform. He had a grenade in the console and an AK 47 on the back seat of the Toyota Camry. He smiled widely and told me what to do in case of emergency, "Don't worry, I think no problem, but if problem, maybe lie down in car and I shoot the gun. Or I throw the grenade."

At Ream, the students were mostly nice people, and protective of me. A younger man asked me if "pillow talk" was the best way to learn a language. He constantly made sexual remarks, some of which were funny in awkward English. I couldn't laugh as it would have encouraged more of the same. I couldn't just be sarcastic, which doesn't work well with language learners because then you have to explain why you said the opposite of what you meant.

I stared at him and said, "Stop talking now. Thank you." That didn't work very well. The other students rolled their eyes and shook their heads when he talked. One day, he asked me, "Teacher, you know the sad thing about nuns?" He said, "They never know the 'joy' of marriage."

In Khmer language, the word "joy" is the equivalent of "fuck," so he was either clever or repeating an old joke. I stared at him, mildly annoyed. Several men in class muttered and looked angry, and said he was no good. A few days later, the highest ranking officer of the student group told me that the jokester was moved to a remote island outpost and would be there for until English lessons were finished.

I focused on long, deep breaths to keep from fainting while teaching at Ream. I finally told Sebastian and Ken that I would finish out the term at Ream, and that was it. As it turns out, it was the final term anyway, so we didn't need to worry about it.

One of the perks of working at ACE School in Sihanoukville was the flight to the capital city, Phnom Penh, once per term. Sihanoukville was a slow-paced place to live, quiet with limited opportunities. We couldn't wait to fly to the capital and check our mailbox, go out drinking at the Heart, and see our friends at ACE Phnom Penh. We had a rough first flight up to Phnom Penh, though.

We'd hired a taxi to drive us to the tiny Sihanoukville airport, but when he overshot it, we realized he was driving up Route 4 to take us to the airport in Phnom Penh. He'd misunderstood us. Now, we could get kidnapped. It was shortly after the three western men were kidnapped and murdered, so our fears were justified. We didn't speak Khmer yet, which made communication nearly impossible. I started hyperventilating while trying to get the driver to stop. Ken said, "Stop talking. Let me do this." He pointed at the brake, and repeated and gestured to stop, repeatedly. Maybe the word "stop" sounded enough like *chhop,* the Khmer word for stop, that the driver finally understood.

The driver turned his Toyota Camry around to head back to the little airstrip. The small Russian plane with round windows was just starting to taxi for take off, but we went squirreling in, kicking up dust. The small plane slammed on the brakes, opened the door, and a little hatch opened and the ladder dropped. As we boarded, out of breath and sweaty, we could hear the French people on board muttering, "Americans." Sheesh!

When we got to Phnom Penh, we settled in at Hotel La Paillote. Then, we were off to Bert's Books for conversation and to buy books, and next, the post office to use the tiny brass key to unlock our drawer and get letters from our parents and friends. We went to the riverfront to eat at the FCCC and watch the Tonle Sap flow, and Lucky's Supermarket for cheese and yoghurt to take back. We went by ACE in Phnom Penh to hang out with our teacher friends and talk about our life in Sihanoukville. They weren't envious. Living in the provinces for more than a few months was hard for people.

After a good time in Phnom Penh, Ken, Sebastian and I ended up on the Russian aircraft flying from Phnom Penh to Sihanoukville. Sebastian went to talk with the pilot before takeoff, and when he returned to his seat near ours, he had a smug look on his face. We asked him what he'd talked about with the pilot.

"I informed the pilot in *no uncertain terms* that I *absolutely* did not want him flying low, just above the ocean, which is something he does. Just make a normal landing, I told him."

Ken and I looked at each other, raising eyebrows, shocked at Sebastian's audacity. We were in for a ride. You just don't tell ex-military how to fly their planes. Sure enough, when we approached Sihanoukville, the pilot suddenly executed a hard bank, putting the passenger aircraft on one ear. We heard the other passengers gasp and I was terrified, but we'd predicted this. From the left side of the plane, we looked out our windows at the ocean below, and up to the right of the plane to see passengers clinging to their arm rests.

The pilot righted the plane and flew just above the ocean, skimming the whitecaps. Sebastian jumped to his feet to go give the pilot "what for." Ken and I made a grab for him, grasping his leather belt and pulling him down into his seat. We landed a few minutes later, and the Khmer pilot smiled and winked at me, tipping his pilot's cap. We razzed Sebastian about that incident for as long as we worked with him. We never flew the same flight with him again.

One night, Ken, Sebastian, and I went out to one of the outside beach restaurants. Claude, a French-Vietnamese man, owned it along with his girlfriend, who he later married. He had a handsome, chiseled face, and she was fair-skinned with thick, straight brown hair. They both spoke many languages, and were well regarded in the community. The food he served was the finest French cuisine, and we liked to spend time there. First, we'd have drinks at the robber's bar, a shellacked wooden, upside-down longboat. The owner explained robbers had stolen it from him, but he stole it back. Then, we moved to a table overlooking the beach washing in and out. The night sky was loaded with stars and light music played, something in French language. None of the mind-jangling disco.

Food there was spectacular—sashimi with soy sauce and ginger, steaks and pork with rich sauces of various types, and drinks served freely—aperitif, wine, digestif. Claude's hosting was the best I've ever encountered, and his girlfriend Bich spoke French, English, Khmer and Vietnamese. She cooked the food.

One night, we were having roast boar with mixed salad, side plates of crudités—crisp pickles and vegetables in a dipping sauce, and plenty of wine. A car pulled up at a nearby restaurant. Two well-dressed Cambodian men pulled another man out of the trunk, and Ken and I, along with Sebastian, began quietly swearing and exclaiming. A man was being *pulled from the trunk.* He seemed lethargic and heavy, a large man.

"Oh, my God. Do you *see* that?" I whispered to the server. She glanced up, then quickly down. She continued pouring wine. My stomach churned. Ken and I watched as one man pulled a gun, and we got behind the robber's bar, ducking. Sebastian joined us. One gunshot rang out, but was oddly silenced—a staccato punch. We were entirely unnerved at this point. The two men lifted the third man, placing him back in the trunk. Some shrubs gave us cover, along with the Robber's Bar. The trunk slammed shut. They got in, backed up and drove away.

"Did you see that? Someone just got shot!" I whispered again to the waitress, who was putting the wine behind the bar, moving gracefully by us. No one at the restaurant said a word. Other diners continued eating. Nothing had been seen. People talked and laughed. The beachside murder simply hadn't occurred. We returned to our table, appetites ruined, paid, and left.

The next day, Ken and I agreed that we shouldn't get involved in the politics of Cambodia.

"We can't go to the police," Ken said.

"That villa must belong to a higher up."

"They'll want money. They won't deal with it anyway."

"Or they'll give us a problem," I said.

"We just need to stay out of politics." Ken was right. We'd been there long enough to see how ineffective the police force was. The next morning, we went to school and taught our classes. Part of living in the Kingdom of Cambodia in 1995 included completely ignoring a horrible occurrence, and then questioning, did that happen?

13

Maids and Ghosts

In Sihanoukville, we needed to find a place to live, and according to Sebastian, we needed a maid. In the U.S., I worked full-time and did all my own housework, as most of us poor young Americans did. Ken did plenty too. I'd never had a maid or worker. In fact, I worked as a maid during college. I didn't mind it, as long as there was some food in the house I was cleaning.

Even while we traveled, and in our first six weeks in Phnom Penh, I hand-washed our clothes and hung them outside to dry. For meals, we ate at restaurants or bought eggs and bread, keeping our diets simple. The Asian markets were the place to go for fresh meat and produce. I bought longan berries with their brown, paper-like shells; the bristled, crimson rambutans; mangoes, pineapples, coconuts, and jackfruit. I didn't buy meat, with pig heads sitting on elevated market stands and cuts of meat drawing copious flies.

Even now, some of the westerners living in Cambodia tell me that extra people from the countryside turn up at their homes, sisters or cousins of their wives. They pick up a broom or help cook and earn some money and eat, have a roof over their heads downstairs in a hammock. It's mutually beneficial. I've lived poor, but poor in a developing country is a completely different situation. People die of hunger. They die of diarrhea. Poverty in Cambodia is a much worse circumstance than poverty in a developed country.

We needed help. Buying food at the Cambodian markets was hard for me. I knew how to speak Khmer language before I could listen and understand it, so my bargaining wasn't good.

"Tlie ponmaan?" I'd ask. The seller would look at me and rattle off a price, and I'd stare blankly. Finally, I'd hold out two-thousand riels and point at what I wanted, and the sellers helped me. They made extra money from me, no doubt. If I held out a ten-thousand riel note, sometimes I got much more food than we needed.

We just didn't have the hours necessary to buy, clean, and cook food. A maid could do our laundry, go to the market, and cook. She could also keep our home tidy. In Cambodia, many young and middle-aged women (and men) lacked education, money, and a means to move forward. We needed to hire someone to help us, and it would be good for her and us. I swallowed my apprehension and we agreed to hire someone.

In post UNTAC Cambodia, wages in the country for unskilled Khmer workers were about $30.00 per month for long hours. Typically, families shared a roof, and pitched in their earnings to survive. Sebastion told us most westerners were paying $30.00 to $40.00 per month for a worker who came in for a short period of time daily. We didn't just want a cleaner, though. We wanted someone who could shop the local markets and cook, and we definitely wanted someone who could help us navigate the culture.

We decided to pay $100.00 per month. There were two of us, anyway. We figured she would spend most of the day at our house, and we wanted to be fair. Sebastian strongly recommended his cleaner Polly. He felt guilty about going back to Holland and leaving her without a job, especially as she was providing for her young daughter. Her two older boys lived with their father, who had left her for a second wife.

Polly told us all about her family. One day, she said,

"I have baby."

"You have baby?" I said, shocked.

"*Kon bi. Muy, pi, bi,*" she said. "One, two, three." She showed me with three fingers. She had three children. The youngest was her daughter, Srey Mum, who lived with grandmother. This took lots of time to understand, as I didn't speak Khmer (Cambodian language). I asked her to bring Srey Mum to meet us, if she wanted.

Polly brought her seven-year-old daughter to our little apartment in Sihanoukville, and I adored her. She was tiny, with shiny black hair and brown eyes, wearing a blue checked dress with flowers on it. She greeted me with a *sampei*, the hands held to the nose showing respect.

She won my heart right away.

Polly told me that in Cambodia there are three kinds of beautiful. The first is unmistakable, perfect beauty. The second is similar to being pretty. And the third, she said, is when you look at someone and can't figure out why they're attractive. You realize that they are beautiful, but you're not sure why.

She said that was Srey Mum's kind of beauty. Srey Mum loved to laugh and was very bright. Ken and I treated her like a daughter, and when we moved to Phnom Penh, she became a part of the family there. Polly and Srey Mum lived with us from 1996 through 2001.

I was "Ma ti pi," Mother number two. Ken was Father. I loved buying Srey Mum clothes and treats, and we sent her to good schools. She went to Khmer school, to Chinese school, to English school. She came home and ate, then got cleaned up and was out the door. She learned quickly. I talked with her constantly, and her English became good.

Polly's two sons lived with their father. He had a building company somewhere south of Phnom Penh. The boys were often over, so we got to know them too.

Polly had a musical voice, capable of expressing great emotion. Once, I stood on the balcony of an apartment Ken and I rented. It was early evening, and the cicadas hummed and resonated faster and higher until I felt my brain was humming, too. A banana tree grew just down the block, its leaves hanging languidly and innocently down in the twilight.

"See that tree?" asked Polly. "I saw a man hanging from a banana tree just like that during Pol Pot."

I said, "What?" and she said it again. I shook my head and said; "no good, no good," clucking my tongue as I'd heard her do so many times.

Polly turned and walked into the apartment, pulling a short broom with wispy straws from the corner. With one hand placed on the small of her back in traditional cleaning posture, she swept the room slowly but methodically. She flipped a cockroach on its back and swept it into the corner, where it lay with its legs twitching. Then she went into the kitchen and began frying fish in the wok, the oil sizzling with a loud crackle when the fish went in.

Ken and I thought we'd teach Polly to speak English. In fact, she taught us Khmer—cheerfully repeating words until we learned them. She was with us for all the time I lived in Cambodia. We loved her, going to her family's house, getting to know her kids, and telling her about our families. She also taught us about the "spirit world" in Cambodia, and kept an eye out for our safety. When someone drove a nail into the doorjamb entering our home, she removed it. Bad luck. When I showed her the photo of an owl, and said it symbolized wisdom, she stared hard at me, and said, "Oh, no—it symbolizes death."

One of our young adult students in Sihanoukville died of electrocution. With cables looped over his head and around his armpit, he climbed a ladder to do some wiring. He was discovered hours later, on the floor dead. Polly reminded me of a premonition the day before.

The young father had held his baby, who would not stop crying. The mother nursed the child, used a washcloth on its bottom, and burped it. When she handed the baby back to her father, the baby again began screaming, inconsolable. When Polly came to tell us of our student's death, she dropped her voice low and asked,

"Do you remember the baby crying yesterday? Crying, crying, would not stop?" We nodded.

Polly said, "The baby knew." It became a catchphrase for Ken and me, when we discussed the unexplainable in Cambodia. The baby knew. Even the sound of a baby crying made Ken and I glance at each other.

While we lived in Sihanoukville, we made friends with Khmer people who asked to be private students. We exchanged thirty minutes of lessons in English for thirty minutes of lessons in Khmer. In time, we heard many stories about ghosts. Ken's teacher told one story, and he wrote it down for me so I'd remember it.

Dear Deb,

You asked about Pheng's Khmer Rouge story…So, in short, Pheng was from Kampong Cham but in 1975 was working in Kampong Thom at the ministry. His family was still in the village in Kampong Cham. He considered himself an educated person and an atheist. Not a casual one, but somebody who had considered and rejected the notion of the supernatural.

When Phnom Penh fell, the Khmer Rouge ordered all personnel from his ministry to assemble at a particular spot at the edge of town, which they did. They were told that they were free to bring their work and personal property with them, as if they were being relocated.

Once there with his co-workers, Pheng got a bad feeling that something was amiss, though he couldn't quite put his finger on it. He made an excuse to one of the cadres there that he needed to go back to the ministry to pick up his work, and they let him go. He only went a few hundred meters, ducked into a gully and made his way to a hollow tree where he hid. A couple of hours later, more soldiers arrived at the meeting point and proceeded to kill everybody there. There were no survivors except Pheng hiding in the tree.

Then he spent 3-1/2 years in Kampong Thom pretending to be a bumpkin toiling in the usual way for peasants under the Khmer Rouge. The Vietnamese invaded, the regime fell, and all the guards and soldiers where he was working abandoned their posts and fled. Like so many Cambodians at that particular moment, the middle of January 1979, Pheng decided to try to walk home, which would be hundreds of miles across a war zone. He had no idea how to get home except to start heading east, which he did. Weeks later, half starved and lost, he was ready to give up, when he met a strange old man on the road. He told the man his village name. The man told him to get off the road, that there were soldiers ahead, and directed him into the jungle, saying his village was that way. As he walked away, he turned back to say something to the old man, but he was gone. Pheng reluctantly entered the jungle and became even more disoriented. He spotted a misty blue light ahead, thought it might be a village and headed for it, but it kept moving away from him. He began to believe that it was guiding him, and for lack of any other options, followed it. He came to a river, which he thought was too deep to cross, and thought about trying to make his way to a nearby bridge that he feared might have soldiers guarding it. In indecision, he rested at the side of a pond on the river where the blue light hovered above the water. The blue light floated toward him and then went back out over the water. Unable to swim and for fear of trying to cross the river, he decided to make for the bridge. When he did, the light did not follow.

As he moved farther away, it just stayed there above the water. He decided this was a sign that the light didn't want him to go to the bridge. He went back to the water's edge, and the light moved farther out onto the water. In faith, he followed it, walking deeper and deeper into the water until almost at nose level. But it got no deeper and he made it to the other side. He prayed to thank the light, now convinced this was a spirit.

The light moved off into the jungle and he followed it for another couple of days. As they reached a clearing the light disappeared, and he found himself just a couple of kilometers from his old village. There, he found his wife, still alive and well enough. Their young daughter was long dead. But he was home. And has been a believer ever since.

Love,

Ken

We learned a lot in Sihanoukville about Khmer culture, not just about ghosts and superstitions, but also how to order food, how to avoid offending people, and how to speak the Khmer language. I learned to dance at weddings, and loved doing Khmer dancing at Colaap I, a local nightclub. Cambodians have an unusual dance, called the Romvong. Men and women dance in a circle, with elaborate hand gestures. Polly told me to think of picking flowers as I danced. Ken preferred sitting and watching the women dance. There were many to watch at Colaap I, about a hundred tiny women mostly from Vietnam. My Dutch friend and her husband went out dancing with us, but she didn't like it there. She worried about her marriage in this country of young, single women everywhere. I didn't worry at all.

14

$\mathcal{D}$octor in the House

Sebastian went back home to the Netherlands, and Ken was promoted to branch manager of Sihanoukville ACE. One week, Ken attended a meeting in Phnom Penh. I stayed behind in Sihanoukville. While he was gone, Polly said Rhatha, a friend of hers, was ill. She'd never get married, said Polly. A young death was imminent. I pulled Ken's copy of *Where There is No Doctor* off the shelf, and started asking questions, but we really needed Rhatha there.

"Bring her over tomorrow," I suggested. Perhaps we could figure out what Rhatha's illness was. The next day, Polly and Rhatha arrived. She wore a scarf around her neck, covering herself up. I pulled out the book, and the three of us sat down at the kitchen table. She unwrapped the scarf and I saw the carbuncles. I'd never in my life used that word, but I knew it. The infected boils covered her neck and chest, and she was uncomfortable, embarrassed, and exhausted. Using the *Where There is No Doctor* book, I worked my way through the questions. Swelling? Yes. Inflammation and infection? I reached the diagnosis: *Lymphatic Tuberculosis*. Now I was nervous. My heart raced. What had I done, thinking I could help? Had I brought disease into our home? I stood up and smiled, telling Rhatha and Polly that I understood the problem now.

"Tomorrow, meet at the hospital at 9 a.m.," I said. Polly showed her to the door, then came back. We used bleach and water to clean the table, then we sat in the living room. Polly knew what tuberculosis was, but we spoke different languages. Now I understood. The problem wasn't identifying the disease. Rhatha needed help to get the donated medicine without having to pay for it.

Polly and I understood each other. Not perfectly, and it took a long time. Polly explained there was a free program for people with tuberculosis, but at the hospital, a worker was demanding money for it. Rhatha couldn't afford it. The staff at the hospital didn't get paid. They earned money by selling donated medications. It was extortion, but it was how Cambodia operated. Free medicines donated to a clinic with unsalaried workers pretty much ensured the outcome.

Polly and I went to the hospital with Rhatha. The dirty black and white tiles in the front were splattered with old blood, dried dark brown patches. A dusty desk stood near the entrance. A child cried from inside. The person working at the front waved his hands when we asked for the free medicine.

"No medicine today. Tomorrow have." A woman walked out with a naked baby with diarrhea. She straddled it over a forearm, wiping its butt with a krama, the ubiquitous blue or red checked scarf people use in Cambodia. Head wrap, neck protector, sarong, baby-butt wiper. The krama is everywhere.

We left and stood outside in the glaring sun. Rhatha said that unless someone gave money to the worker, he said "no medicine." She was exhausted, and I told her to go rest. We agreed to meet again at the hospital the next morning. I asked Polly where the director of the hospital lived, and she took me to his house. We went with motodops, and she left me at his front door.

"Sorry, I need to go," said Polly. She was clearly nervous about going inside with me, and it was getting late in the morning. Work was always best done early. She needed to go to the market and shop for dinner. In front of the hospital director's white cement house were gigantic Century Fan palms to either side. Purple Bougainvillea blossoms cascaded down from pots on floors above, and a trickling fountain stood by the side of a large, carved mahogany door. I smoothed my hair back with both hands, securing it with an elastic band I kept on my wrist. I'd be teaching in an hour, so I was wearing a long dress and simple earrings.

A woman answered the door and ushered me in. She beckoned me to a huge, intricately carved wooden chair, a highly glossed mahogany-colored wood with white stripes. Flowers and trees were carved into the back of it, and the huge arm rests curled downward. On a matching coffee table, four plane tickets to Los Angeles from

Phnom Penh were fanned out on display. The trip was for the following week. When the director walked in, I stood and gave a respectful *sampei* greeting, hands in prayer and held lightly to the bowed head. The more respect, the higher the *sampei*. He greeted me and we sat. He spoke English pretty well, and we talked briefly about his upcoming trip. He was taking his family to Disneyland.

The opulence of the surroundings contrasted with the filth of the hospital. I presented my case. My friend was ill. Medicine was supposed to be free. The hospital personnel were selling, and she couldn't afford the medication. The director assured me he'd take care of the situation. Then, I paused.

"Everyone with tuberculosis needs the free medicine." I glanced at the tickets to the U.S. and allowed my eyes to linger for just a moment. I imagined all of the thousands of dollars coming in from donor countries, while the Khmer people suffered with tuberculosis and tolerated the filthy hospital, while the director and his family planned their trip to Disneyland in California.

He escorted me to the door. I had classes to teach, and felt dizzy. I had giardia, and eating gave me horrible cramps, so I avoided solid food. By drinking coconut water straight from the coconut, I avoided exposure to more unsanitary water. I got a motodop and headed to school. I needed to rest for a few minutes and sip the fluid, the only thing that helped me to feel better.

My health was not great. I measured my life in school terms. Maybe if I could get through the term, I'd find a doctor who could help me. I took medicine for what felt like forever. Maybe I needed yoghurt. Weight was falling off me. I tried to sit while I was teaching, so I wouldn't faint. I breathed slowly, willing oxygen to circulate through my body. Years later, I read in Ken's journal how worried he was about me. He didn't show it at the time. Eventually, I got stronger. So did Rhatha.

When I saw Rhatha after a year, I couldn't believe my eyes. She was nicely dressed—no more giant scarf—her glossy hair was secured in a ponytail, and her eyes looked good. Her skin, while scarred, was clear. Her wedding was planned for an auspicious date a few months later.

15

Flesh and Bones

We taught all of 1995 and most of 1996 in Sihanoukville, getting to know every expat in the community—perhaps ten. We made friends with Tim, a U.S. ex-military man of perhaps thirty, and his Vietnamese wife Toy. He'd met her at Colaap I, a local nightclub filled with perhaps a hundred Vietnamese and Khmer girls there every night. Polly said they were taxi girls (prostitutes). She said they were called that because they could sit on taxis and go home with people. I think the other place we went to for dancing and people-watching was Whiskey-a-Go-Go, a smaller place with good music and more taxi girls.

Toy was beautiful, and Tim said she was the girl he'd always dreamed of. The other men in the community raised eyebrows. They'd known her long before Tim met her. Tim pampered her, handing over large sums of money and encouraging her to treat herself at the beauty parlor and market. She invited me to the beauty parlor with her, where the beauticians washed our hair while we were sitting up, just adding more water and soap and massaging shampoo in. She sat still with her eyes closed, like a tiny satisfied cat.

"Everything I do is for a beautiful face and a beautiful body," she said. "I exercise for beauty." I didn't share her focus on beauty. As long as I stayed skinny with long hair, Ken was happy with my looks.

Her fixation on her appearance seemed over the top, but she'd landed Tim. She bought little-girl outfits—sailor girl and cheerleader, to name a few. I couldn't relate, and Ken and I were amused with her expenditures and Tim's fascination with her.

Finally, crisis hit. Toy was in Vietnam visiting her family. When she returned, she examined the sheets of their conjugal bed. A black pubic hair was detected. Tim's hair was light brown. With the

certainty of a forensic detective, Toy presented the hair to Tim.
Things got messy fast, and her crying and yelling played out in public.
Tim appeared around town with swollen eyes and a gloomy
expression. Toy might leave him.

In time, Toy made Tim move, buy a new bed, and get
counseling. Tim had to swear an oath to never cheat again. All of us
gossiped constantly about each other, and this was juicy stuff. We
wondered if Tim had actually cheated, or if he was just confessing to
salvage their marriage. Later on, Toy moved her seven-year-old son
from Vietnam (from another relationship). He started spitting on
other kids, and I had to give him a little talk. Toy came to pick him
up from school that day, and he ran to her and whispered to her. She
walked fast to one of the Khmer boys, an eight-year-old, and started
shaking him and screaming. When I intervened, she said, "He kick
my son in the balls! Cause big problem with health!"

"No," I said. "He got in trouble for spitting." Her kid's
maneuver was a diversionary tactic, and I'd seen it before. While our
school was full of really nice kids and adults, the new boy caused
problems. I figured it had to do with his mom, who was always
scheming. Eventually, the family left town. Ken and I were relieved,
as the dramas at school became uncomfortable.

Our friend Chris, British ex-military opened the Angkor Arms
pub with three other partners—Tony, Arrun, and a Singaporean. A
Dutch couple worked near the hospital as physical therapists, and a
British fellow and an Irish man made prosthetic limbs. Someone was
volunteering to teach English in a British program, and there was an
Italian-Australian entrepreneur who sang karaoke with us. He turned
in his song requests, and if the worker didn't play his song fast
enough, he threw a fit.

"Hey, fuck head. Yeah, you. When's my song going to play?"

"Oh, Mr. Tony! Your song! One moment." The Khmer workers
knew Tony well. Tony would hold a hundred-dollar bill up high,
showing them. Other singers belted out "Love Me Tender" or
something by Karen Carpenter. If the song didn't end in half a
minute, the bill was ripped over and over again, and Tony stomped

to the door, his girlfriend rolling her eyes in frustration at Tony, shaking her head, the "no good" gesture women share when men are difficult. Ken and I apologized for Tony and watched the Khmers in the office meticulously taping the money.

We shared uneasy amusement at Tony's temper, and agreed it was a problem, but Ken admired him and enjoyed watching his girlfriend. Tony was good-looking and muscular, and his Vietnamese girlfriend was beautiful with shiny, thick hair hanging straight to her hips. When we went out to sing, she sat near him, playing with his hair or massaging his shoulders. When she walked, her long, straight hair came alive, cascading around her body in a shiny waterfall.

At that time, people didn't dare travel Route 4 because of the Khmer Rouge, so we didn't get visitors. One time flying back from Phnom Penh, a physical therapist brought his sister to visit. When we exited the plane, she immediately fainted. She was terrified to be there. We westerners living in Sihanoukville were a close group of people and spent time having dinners, playing board games, or gossiping about each other. It was good to talk with people who shared a common language. Even if our politics were different, we could at least talk.

At home, Ken and I studied Khmer language, read a lot of books, and watched movies on a small television. Ken bought the VHS movies down at the market, as I couldn't stand dealing with the lecherous middle-aged Chinese seller who tried to sell me porn videos. He had a hairy mole on his face that he'd pull with his fingers, staring at me as he held up a VHS tape cover of a woman copulating with a dog. I shook my head and said, "No good," and walked away as he smiled.

At sunset, Ken and I rode his motorcycle to the top of Victory Hill in Sihanoukville, and watched the boats coming in from the ocean. He loved the twinkling lights that flickered on the ocean's rounded horizon, like diamonds glittering around the moon during a solar eclipse.

Sihanoukville was a quiet place with fresh seafood and warm ocean waters. Sokha Beach was only a few minutes away, and we both had motorcycles. I'd gotten good on my Honda Dream, and rode it too fast. Ken and I rode to Sokha Beach, to Ochateal Beach, and Otres Beach. He loved to go to Otres and sit on the beach with me. Rarely was anyone ever on that beach. We took cold drinks with us in a little insulated bag. I'd strip down to my light blue swimsuit and jump around in the surf. Ken asked me not to go to that beach without him, as it was isolated.

I'd gone alone once. I was lying on my side near the sea reading, absentmindedly brushing sand off my butt when I heard above me, "L'aa!"-- which in Khmer language is not a "nice girl" compliment, but sexual in some contexts, according to Polly. It means *good* in an Austin Powers way, "Yeah, baby. Good." I looked up to see an overweight Khmer guy right above me. It was an isolated beach in those days. I jumped up and yelled at him to go away.

One day, I was in the kitchen at our apartment in Sihanoukville when Ken came in with an excited look on his face.

"Well," he said. "Something interesting seems to be going on at the beach." There was seldom interesting news, and when news did come, it was a death, an accident, or something political from Phnom Penh. We even got our *Cambodia Daily* newspapers late down there. *The Phnom Penh Post* might appear within a week of its publication, or it might not.

"A fisherman's body has been spotted in the sea, and it is washing onto the beach, then being carried out again."

"Oh, great." I wasn't interested in this story yet. "Did you go down there?"

"No. But I think I will and see what's going on." Ken asked me to go, but I was getting more than enough exposure to tragedies in Cambodia without gawking at a drowned fisherman.

Ken was back in about an hour, leaving his sandy tennis shoes at the door. He had a tale to tell.

"Japanese tourists are down there filming it with their video cameras, and Collin and I thought it was disrespectful to the dead, so we got the police to come down!"

This story was gaining momentum. The police could be counted on to do nothing, or to try and extort money from someone at the scene. As soon as they entered any narrative, my ears pricked up. Ken knew he'd hooked me.

"The police looked, and said, 'dead,' and then they just left!" Of course they left! While a corpse in the water might be disturbing to authorities in many countries, a corpse in Cambodia could mean only one thing: late to dinner with wet shoes.

Collin and Ken collected the bits and pieces of the fisherman— he was breaking up fast—and buried him up by a palm tree, deep into the sandy soil. That was where Ken saw his first offering to *Ya Mao*. When he saw the phallus, he pointed it out to Collin, who asked, "Never seen one of those, mate?"

Ya Mao is a "spirit" guardian of the Southern Cambodia area. Her husband was a fisherman working on one of the islands, and one day she missed him so she took a boat to spend some time with him. On the way, a storm came up, overturning the boat. Ya Mao drowned. Over time, people came to believe that she was a guardian spirit of that area. At Pich Nil, on the way down Route 4, spirit houses full of hand-made phalluses line the road. Ya Mao is older now, it is said, so offering her fruit is fine (especially bananas). When it became safe to travel on Route 4, Ken and I took bananas to Ya Mao on our way north to Phnom Penh. Once, I pulled a carved wooden phallus out of my pocket to offer her. He said, "Where did you get that?" It had come from Russian Market, I think. I'd bought it to make him smile, and it worked.

16

Angkor Wat

"Some anthropologists like stones, some like bones. You know I studied anthropology for a while, right? I like stones. You won't believe it up there. The temples are practically empty, just little kids and monks. There are so many. You're going to love it," Ken said. I was eager to go, but we had a school term to get through first.

We went to Angkor Wat together in March 1995. That month begins the hot season in Cambodia. To see the sunrise, we were up early, and it was chilly. For the sunset at Phnom Bakheng, the climb up the hill was steep and hot. The climb down was hard.

There's a camaraderie that develops with people descending slowly. The Khmer women put out their hands to me, smiling and nodding. I've never been good with coming downhill. Khmer men generally won't touch a woman in public, unless the woman is their wife. Grandmothers and parents and children descended together.

"Sometimes, we come only one time in our life," one girl told me. "It's very expensive for us." I felt guilty about the disparity. For us, it was an easy-to-afford trip. This was so special to the Cambodians, not just a place to check out, but of huge religious importance to them. They were Buddhists. Angkor Wat was the most famous temple of all.

One afternoon at 4 p.m., we were at Angkor Wat. We walked around the lower level with the bas reliefs (raised carvings), which told stories of war, conquest, daily life, and, also, of the cosmos. On the east wall, perhaps the most famous bas relief tells the story of creation itself, with the "Churning of the Ocean Milk" bas relief. Ken and I loved this wall. Apsaras, Cambodian "angels," rise from the churning, up to the top of the carving.

Black clouds rolled in, and a fast drop in the temperature occurred. I was on the west side of the enclosed stone temple, walking and studying the art of the bas reliefs, meandering along and enjoying the heady aroma of bat shit. I was alone, without even a nun nearby. I stood in a rectangular stone doorway, looking toward the open field to see two monks in bright orange robes trotting away. The rain was so hard that it created the effect of a hazy curtain, and it struck the ground outside in the crescendo of a hard downpour.

This was like my home state of Oregon, with its lush green grass and hard rain storms. I stood and watched. I stood on a giant stone slab, the day's heat warming my bare feet. After some time, I walked slowly along the next wall. Images of men with swords on horses marched along beside me. As I turned the corner to the east wall, there was Ken. I watched him for some time. He looked up at the wall, then wrote in his journal.

I sat with him. We shared some water, and he combed my long hair, which got tangled riding motorcycles. We waited on the rain before heading back to Siem Reap.

Ken and I went to Angkor Wat more times than I can count. I've wandered among the giant faces of Bayon, and sipped on fresh coconuts around the temples. I've been there when it's so hot the air seemed to radiate. We looked for the parrots at the jungle temple of Ta Prohm, not quite able to see the bright green birds although we could hear them.

We had our favorite temples. We both liked Prey Rup, which a nearby sign interpreted as "turn the body." Some thought it to be a funeral temple, but it wasn't. Still, the name fascinated us, and we liked the tall mountain temples best. Prey Rup climbed up to the sky. It was remote and fewer people tended to show up.

We rode motorcycles from temple to temple, paying people to watch them for us. We kept notes as we toured, and compared ideas and impressions. At night, we lay in bed and talked. One of us would comment on the Terrace of the elephants, and the other would answer with a detail about Ta Prohm, the jungle temple. Then, we'd breathe quietly and fell asleep.

The temples are set among vines and trees that grow curving among the ruins. Monkeys live around Bayon Temple with its gigantic carved faces. I was at the Phnom Penh ACE school and overheard an administrator on the phone with the manager of the Siem Reap branch. A teacher had been warned to leave the monkeys alone, but he got a fairly deep bite. He had to go through the rabies vaccines in Phnom Penh, and the administrator was annoyed.

More than once, I saw a tourist hand a banana to a small monkey. Within seconds, the pack beset the tourist, climbing her body and taking *all* of the bananas, along with her necklace and sunglasses. In Cambodia, a cluster of bananas is called a "hand," and I've seen a group of monkeys fighting tooth and nail to get the entire hand away from the tourists. We sat on our motorcycles far away from the naïve travelers and watched them get mauled.

"We warned them," we'd say, laughing a little. We stayed our distance.

Ken and I got to know the children of Angkor Wat quite well, and Ken helped Leo, one of the poor children who stayed at Angkor Wat who sold trinkets and bracelets. Leo was small, with big ears and sad eyes. He always wore the same ripped shirt and dingy black pants. He was barefoot, like all the children there. Ken took me to meet Leo our first time at Angkor Wat. Leo talked in the quietest little voice, and an old nun with a shaved head and white robe looked after him for Ken.

The first time Ken gave Leo some money, the older boys beat him up and stole it. He made an arrangement with the nun. She took care of Leo and she held the money, so the little boy wouldn't get beaten and robbed. When Leo got ill, Ken helped buy good medicine. Often, charlatan doctors give patients one blue pill, one red pill, and some aspirin. Ken worked out how to help Leo.

In time, the sellers of the temples knew us, and whether or not we wanted a cold drink or snack, we always purchased an item. The sellers depended on buyers, and they were very poor. We often spent sunset at Angkor Wat, as it was cool on a hot day, and we didn't want to climb up Phnom Bakheng. I took my shoes off and walked barefoot, soaking up the warmth of the stones through the soles of my feet. On a hot day, the stone floor inside the temples was cool.

Stone was worn smooth from centuries of bare feet. People loved the apsaras—the carved angel women. The stone carvings of apsaras depict young women wearing long skirts. They are bare from the hips up, and their flat bellies and round breasts are rich and glossy from centuries of people touching the stone.

In time, the Khmer children at the temples showed us the special apsaras at Angkor Wat, like the one with the forked tongue. People who listened to the children got tours. Of course, we were buying their little bracelets too. Our favorite carvings were of two apsaras who were friends. We always visited them, something of a ritual for Ken and me. The two apsaras are on an inner wall, and they're hard to photograph, as an opposing wall blocks the shot. They are smiling, and one has her arm around the other's waist. Ken and I thought they were real, living people at some point in time. The carver of those particular apsaras was especially gifted. Their faces are beautiful.

In September, I turned thirty-six in Sihanoukville. That morning I woke up unhappy. I felt sluggish, and my eyes were swollen. I'd had bad dreams all night. I had wanted to have a baby by thirty-five. No baby, and no discussion. As always, I didn't bring it up with Ken. Maybe I assumed Ken could read my mind. One thing was for sure. He knew my birthday wasn't going well.

Ken insisted we go to the market. He wanted to buy me a gold chain. I didn't want to go. He pushed and pushed, gently asking me to go with him. Finally, he went alone and bought me a necklace. I remember this birthday as one of the unhappiest I've ever had.

17

*C*anby Publications

We quit teaching for ACE school in Sihanoukville in July 1996. We were tired, in part because of the grueling class hours. The Cambodian people and children had jobs and school during the day, so we taught English classes early in the morning and late in the afternoon. Ken and I were thin. The heat, along with frequent stomach problems, had melted our weight off. I looked thin, but Ken was practically skeletal. We planned a trip home to the USA. I wanted to stay there. Ken didn't.

While teaching and managing the Sihanoukville branch of ACE, Ken considered other work. His father had worked with publications, and Ken decided he wanted to publish a guide magazine for Sihanoukville. A Dutch man in Phnom Penh had become a successful publisher. He met with us at the Eagle's Nest on Ochateal beach to explain how he'd done it. First, he'd obtained a college loan. Next, he ran away from his home country. He used the college loan money on his publishing business in Cambodia. I thought this was unscrupulous and wasn't impressed, but Ken admired his ingenuity.

In his free time, Ken began working on a tourist guide for Sihanoukville. He researched constantly, keeping detailed notes about hotels and interesting places around the quiet beach town. He drove all over the area, keeping scaled and detailed sketches. At the end of our time living in Sihanoukville, Ken had lists of hotels with prices, photos, and descriptions, along with a good map.

We were going back to the States to visit our families and travel for at least three months. We'd been overseas for a long time. I would turn thirty-seven in two months, September. I wanted to go home. I didn't trust the politics in Cambodia. Rule of law was pretty much nonexistent. Why set down roots in a country I didn't want to stay in? I no longer thought about trying to have a baby. It was too disappointing. Maybe I'd just wanted to have kids because it was what married people did. Did I even want a baby? It was pretty late in the game for us. For me. Women don't do as well over the age of thirty-five when they try to have babies. I began to feel like it was a lost cause even trying. I was past my expiration date.

In the U.S., we went to see Ken's brother and sister-in-law in Michigan, and they had a beautiful toddler. The brother announced that the wife was again pregnant. Seeing how quiet I got at the inner table when they shared their news, Ken announced to me that night he was ready to have a family. At first I was happy. I wasn't too old! We could certainly try. Maybe it would work.

A few weeks later, I understood Ken's thinking when he explained his idea for our future.

"You can have a baby, and I'll be publishing," he said. A conditional sentence, I thought. The curse of teaching ESL. What he was really saying was, "If you go to Cambodia with *me*, we'll have a baby for *you*."

I said, "Why would you set up a publishing company for just one guide? Do you plan to write guides to Phnom Penh and Siem Reap, and make those maps too? That's going to take a lot of time, a lifetime. Do you want to live out your days in Cambodia?"

He said, "Well, there's a lot of money to be made. Let's see what happens." He knew I didn't want to go back. We were far away from friends and family in a physically challenging place, and cultural differences could be frustrating. I couldn't hike there. It was too hot for me, and besides, I worried about bombs, not unjustifiably. Nor was I enjoying the night life like men do in Southeast Asia.

More than two years had passed already, years away from Oregon, a lush green hiking and biking oasis. Two years away from my parents and friends. Truth be told, I didn't like arguing with Ken, and he always avoided hard discussions. He told me that his parents said "everything's fine" when problems came up. My parents slammed doors and drove off when things got hard. Consequently, we'd be raised in a communication wasteland.

Finally, I said, "I'm done traveling. I want to be in my home state."

Ken said, "I've done all the work. I'd really like to give publishing a try. You won't have to work! You can be a stay-at-home mom. I'll work." I took this in. I'd been working since I was seventeen, and had never let anyone pay my way. Except Dad. Dad sometimes helped me out. I helped him too though. Hadn't I taken care of him for years? I was a worker. Staying at home in Cambodia wasn't a big bonus, not at all. I'd get bored.

He finally won me over, but it wasn't a strong win. I turned thirty-seven in the U.S., and he flew to Cambodia a short time later. I wanted an exam to make sure I was fit to have a baby. I didn't trust the hospitals in Cambodia. A doctor reassured me I seemed healthy. I got back to Cambodia and Ken met me at the airport.

I didn't stop working. I sold ads. The guides were free, so the ads were the only source of revenue. I rode around on Sihanoukville and Phnom Penh on the back of motorcycles under a hot tropical sun for months selling the advertisements. Ken worked on the computer in the hotel.

Sometimes we made love at night, but usually we were too tired. We were trying for a baby, but given our dwindling sex life, it didn't seem to be in the works. We used the money we'd saved to seed Canby Publications. I collected deposits on the advertisements as I sold them. It was hard work. It was hot, dusty outside work riding on a motorcycle going from place to place.

As soon as I'd sold enough ads to afford going to press along with a large profit for us, I went back to teaching for ACE Phnom Penh. Glad to be done with riding on the back of a motorcycle in the sweltering Cambodian heat on dusty roads with potholes, I became the Special Projects Coordinator at ACE Phnom Penh and worked with banks, hospitals, phone companies whose staff needed to learn English.

18

$\mathcal{T}$he Year 1997

One day at Sokha Beach, a handsome young man walked toward me, carrying a big glossy inner tube. He was glistening wet, and his brown skin glowed. The picture of health and vitality, he walked past me, and I focused my Canon AE1 on him. His right arm, muscular and well defined, carried the tube. The photograph was perfect for our first magazine cover. It was also unusual in this country of beautiful women. Here was a photo of a young man walking away. Not a woman. A man.

People around him played, relaxed in the sun, and enjoyed the tropical beach. The circular large inner tube looked great. You can't see the model's face. I did, and he was handsome. Women along the beach turned to watch him as he walked along the sand. Western and Asian men alike looked at our first magazine cover photo and said, "Hey, that's me!"

Ken did the layout, and our printer in Phnom Penh was a professional with a team of workers and big noisy machines that spit out newspapers and magazines. He didn't speak English, but Ken and I communicated with him just fine.

The excitement of having our own publishing company, named Canby Publications after my hometown, was tempered with our worries about the country's stability. We were promoting Cambodia as a tourist destination right around the time the co-prime ministers started having serious problems. The tension in the city was unbelievable. Shop doors were either locked, or the accordion-like metal gates were pulled halfway closed. Ken was tense.

"You have to watch the city. Keep your eyes open. See those gates pulled together, nearly touching? They're not normally closed." Ken pointed out the sand bags set up near politicians' homes.

"Keep out of crowds, stay far away from them." Ken was

adamant. A few bombs went off in the city, and at the site of one, my friend Ellen and I climbed into the crater a few minutes after it had detonated. We'd been drinking at the FCCC and heard the explosion, and drove to the site with a journalist friend. The crater's depth was probably about three feet. We were mentioned in the *Cambodia Daily* article, fortunately not by name.

In Phnom Penh, where the citizens shot at clouds with AK-47's and M-16's, explosions were newsworthy but somewhat normal. Not now, though. These explosions weren't cows stepping on unexploded ordinance in a field somewhere. These explosions were warnings or attacks, the large drops that come just before a monsoon downpour.

Ken and I avoided discussing politics with the Cambodian people. Early on, we adopted a "zero interference" approach. We weren't about to engage Cambodian friends in awkward discussions about politics. Most of them remembered the Khmer Rouge 70s when one word spoken at the wrong time could mean death. That didn't stop us from talking with each other and other foreigners in Cambodia, though. We watched the local politics closely, reading every word of the English language newspapers. The *Cambodia Daily* and *Phnom Penh Post* kept us informed. We discussed politics with our westerner friends nonstop.

We lived in the Hun Sen Compound, not because of our personal politics. We'd found a great apartment there. We were probably surrounded by CPP members, but some other foreigners too. An Australian woman was next door. American attorneys lived on the floor above us. Otherwise, our neighbors were all Cambodian people, mostly Hun Sen's family and bodyguards, I think.

On March 30th, 1997, a major incident occurred a few blocks from our home. Sam Rainsy was running against Hun Sen with the Cambodian People's Party (the CPP) in the election of 1998. Rainsy was a threat because the people liked him. In 1997, Hun Sen had been a prime minister for twelve years.

Ken and I were sleeping in our bedroom, enclosed with thick cement walls, when an explosively loud, reverberating boom woke us both up. I've never experienced anything like it, and I grew up in the countryside of rural Oregon where all of the farmers, including Dad and Grandpa, used explosives to blow up stumps. I felt the concussive noise as much as heard it.

What was that?

I only remember the one huge boom, and then a few smaller noises. Ken went out to investigate. I was getting sick of Cambodia, especially Phnom Penh. The grime, heat, constant dust, and glaring sun were wearing me down. I loved Ken, but I was losing my curiosity and interest. A tragedy? A bomb? A gun? Just one more thing. It wasn't just one more thing, though. Not this time.

The Sam Rainsy political rally had been attacked by someone throwing grenades. Ken came back on his motorcycle, and insisted I go see. People had died, a lot of them.

"Don't worry, they're not there now. This is history. You need to see this."

"I'm not sure I want to."

"This is big. You should see it. Come on." Okay. I could tell he was upset. He liked to discuss events with me; while we didn't talk politics with Cambodians, we talked about them constantly in our home. We read the *Cambodia Daily* newspaper every single day and stayed on top of politics. We had to. It was Cambodia.

I got on the back of Ken's motorcycle, and we rode the short distance, about one minute away on the motorcycle. We drove past the park slowly. It was quiet at the scene. Flip Flops littered the ground like confetti, bits of maroon and navy and white. I'll never forget that. Dark blood stained some parts of the grass, flies buzzing up and settling again. People milled around the perimeter, looking but not talking. Ken and I rode past the park several times, trying to figure out what happened. We joined several Khmer people at the riverfront, and they said there had been bombs at the Sam Rainsy rally. They pointed and said, "Boom!" gesturing with their hands. Several people had died in the explosions.

Those of us who identified as expats or immigrants in Cambodia were shaken up and we sat in bars around town and exchanged what we knew. We heard that a few men were seen running from the attack toward the pagoda just west of the park, into the area of the Hun Sen compound where Ken and I rented an apartment. CPP bodyguards parted to allow the grenade-throwers through the line, according to newspapers, then amassed again, forming a line and keeping their guns ready, not letting people run after the grenade throwers.

Ken and I kept our political opinions to ourselves, but this atrocity was beyond the pale. Hadn't the Khmer people suffered enough? Who was responsible? There was a huge cry for justice from Cambodians and foreigners alike. A jaw-dropping color photograph that I'll never forget covered half of the front page of *The Phnom Penh Post*, taken by journalist Jason Barber. It accompanies an article he wrote with journalist Christine Chaumeau. The photograph bears witness to the horrible, awful truth—that in Cambodia, a ruling government party would attack its own people to maintain power.

The photograph shows a beautiful young woman, a street vendor who probably sold sugar cane juice. The lower-left corner of the photo reveals a beautiful face, knit with concern and confusion— *what's happened to me?* She's young, perhaps a teenager. The top of her body is uncovered, and it appears her clothing has been blown off, except for a bra. One breast is covered in blood. She lifts her hands, imploring someone for help. Perhaps she's trying to move. She is so displayed, this young woman. This goes against Cambodian mores. In the photo, her legs dissolve away, empty space soaked with bright red blood. Her legs are gone. I couldn't stop staring at the photo. The full color photo on the front of *The Phnom Penh Post* rocked the community.

I considered writing *The Phnom Penh Post* to protest their printing it, but realized my anger was misdirected. This act of terrorism made me furious. Sam Rainsy himself would be dead if his bodyguard hadn't thrown himself on top of him. The bodyguard died.

Foreigners in the community kept waiting for something to

come of the investigation. Nothing happened. Then, we heard the FBI was going to investigate. Thank God for that. Time dragged on. Justice deferred. And deferred. Finally, the U.S. Ambassador was questioned. FBI agents working the case stopped. *What?* Apparently, their lives were threatened. So, nothing happened.

Most believed that the entire incident was perpetrated by the Cambodian government, which has received billions of dollars of support from the U.S., Japan, Australia, and many countries around the world. Most also believed that the attack was orchestrated to kill Rainsy, but he survived while innocent people had died.

The Cambodian people whispered the truth: If you oppose the leading party, you'll be eliminated, and no one will do a thing about it. It was a bleak time. So many hopes and promises of a democracy up in smoke. Democracy in Cambodia had been a ruse all along.

In 2019, twenty-two years have passed since the murders of the people—called Bloody Sunday by some and the Day of Impunity by others. While the press is currently severely threatened and in some cases eliminated (*The Cambodia Daily* was closed down recently by the Cambodian government), online sources are alive and well.

What happened to the beautiful girl on the front of *The Phnom Penh Post?* I hoped she was moved to the hospital, attended closely, and then sent somewhere to rehabilitate. I hoped she learned to use a wheelchair, and went on to work as a receptionist at the Cambodiana Hotel, the fanciest place to stay until five-star Hotel InterContinental came along.

She died at the scene. A photo I found online showed her being lifted into a cart.

1997 was getting tense, no doubt about it. One day, a mine-clearing agency—CMAC—detonated some loud bombs outside the city, and people panicked. Cambodians rushed home and pulled their metal accordion-style doors closed, locking them. I was in charge of the school cell phone, and got ahold of a director and administrator, who chided me for panicking.

"Deb, let us check. We'll call you back. Don't panic."

"I'm not panicking. The explosions were loud. Some staff are leaving the school," I said

"Well, don't over-react."

"Um, I'm not. I'm just telling you what's going on."
While I was annoyed, I understood their position. If all the teachers left Cambodia, they'd be out of work. The atmosphere was tense.

One day at ACE school, I was in my office when an American co-worker breezed in with a sheet of paper.

"Hey, I'm leaving country. Politics are getting too stressful for me. Can you take on the U.S. Embassy Warden job?"

"What do I have to do? And what's the pay?"

"It's easy, but no pay. It's a volunteer position. Here's a list of U.S. Citizens you're in charge of. You call them and say hi, introduce yourself, and if there's a big problem—like military action in the city--call and check on them and report back to the American Embassy."

"I don't know. Okay. Sure." I looked at the list. Perhaps a dozen names of U.S. citizens were there, with phone numbers. I took it home and Ken put it with our important documents. The U.S. Embassy called and thanked me for volunteering to be the new warden. Wardens were being prepared for a problem between the prime ministers.

Malgosia, Ken and I were the best of friends in 1996 and 1997. In times of stress, Malgosia found us, or we found her. We loved her outspoken announcements in beautiful, European-accented English, her laugh, and her independent nature. Malgosia was a gifted teacher, and worked in Phnom Penh on various high-stakes language projects. With ACE, she taught Workplace English, and as her program coordinator, I trusted her with any assignment in the business sector.

She got along with the Khmer staff and students. As a child, her family had fled Poland, and they settled in Quebec, Canada. She spoke Polish, English, French, and Khmer—and she spoke the languages well. Everyone liked her.

Malgosia had long legs, which we all admired. She could outride thieves on her dirt bike. She wasn't afraid of long rides either, and drove down Route 4 with Ken, after it was safe. With flyaway blond hair and yellow-green eyes, she'd mount her 250cc motorcycle, start up, and speed away.

On June 17th, 1997, Malgosia came to our apartment in the Hun Sen Compound. I rarely went out at night, but she had invited me to go for a drink. Before leaving the house, I sat in the kitchen talking with Ken and Malgosia. Suddenly I had a terrible pain in my left side, and moved to the floor, stretching out and doing an exam on my left side, feeling the area where it hurt. I was having pains like this often, and had noticed cramping in my left side when I was at the gym. I was doing forty or so sit ups at a time, so maybe it was nothing.

The pain went away, and we left the apartment, Ken telling us to be careful. We got on Malgosia's motorcycle and rode to the Heart of Darkness, where we got drinks and settled in at a small table. A short time later, we began hearing pops, almost like repetitive champagne corks. People in the bar went to the door and looked out. Everything went quiet. The music went off. "It's gunfire," someone said. It was nearby. It seemed to be getting closer.

Malgosia said, "Let's get out of here," and we went to her motorcycle after checking the street. We rode north a short distance and turned right at Street 154 and drove the block to Norodom Boulevard. Military Police were there with AK-47s. One said, "where are you going?" and then he stopped the others from aiming and shooting their machine guns down Norodom, "Stop stop stop." It all happened so fast. He kept us from crossing until his signal, holding us back with one hand. Then, he said, "Go go go go go!" in Khmer, and Malgosia screamed at me to hold on. I was already melded into her, holding on to her waist with my feet on the pedals. She sprang across Norodom Boulevard, gunning it so hard I felt my head jerk backwards. My heart was pounding so I could hear it. Feel it.

Malgosia slowed down after getting us across Norodom, and

pointed out an old Khmer gentleman wearing his red and white checked krama around his waist, standing outside and smiling a toothless grin, waving at us and gripping his AK-47.

"Home protection device, Deb," she said, laughing hard. We were euphoric at having escaped the gunfight.

We continued east to the FCC where journalists stood in the street with cell phones to their ears. They were oblivious to us, two women who had just ridden through the gun fight. They turned to men arriving, asking questions. Phnom Penh was man's land, and we were invisible.

Ken was frantic, answering his phone with "Where are you right now?" and could hardly believe it when I told him we'd ridden through Norodom Boulevard during the fight. He later admitted he was a little jealous too. He loved high-adrenalin adventures. I have to admit that I did too. A week later, I had an adventure that nearly killed me.

When I was eight years old, Mom kept a family medical reference book in a small closet. We lived on a farm, and had occasion to need that medical reference book. As a chubby little kid, I stood in the dim hallway and stared at the sketch of a tiny embryo lodged in a fallopian tube. *An ectopic pregnancy is a cause of death in the first trimester*, the caption read. *It is called a "tubal pregnancy" because the fertilized egg may implant in the fallopian tube. It is nonviable. The mother's life is at risk.* I looked at the page so many times that the book fell open to it. It bothered and fascinated me at the same time.

Thirty years later, I felt ill. It was June 25th, 1997. My lower abdomen was achy, and I couldn't stand up straight. I looked in the bathroom mirror and my face was chalky, almost opaque. I was supposed to teach English at Hotel InterContinental that day. It was a hospitalities English program, administered by ACE Phnom Penh. Ken had stayed up most of the night to burn the Sihanoukville Visitors Guide on cd's for the printer. I'd called in sick the previous week with stomach pain, so I couldn't take another day off. It crossed my mind that it was the anniversary of my brother's last full day alive.

I got into business attire and caught a cyclo. I arrived at the hotel around 9 a.m. with that "sense of impending doom" heart attack victims sometimes report. I was teaching the class when a dull sensation of pain and dizziness washed over me. I could neither stand nor sit. My body told me, "Stop every single thing. Pay attention." It was like a voice.

I excused myself and went to the ladies room. There was bright blood, not the normal rust. I was in trouble. A wave of vertigo hit me, and I breathed slowly, splashing cold water on my face with trembling hands. I returned to the classroom, bent oddly at the waist, and apologized to all. My students' brown eyes showed concern; the Cambodian people understand suffering well, and they could see I was in pain, not *sabay* (happy).

I was pretty sure I was dying in this country with emergency services phone number. Hospitals in Cambodia were abysmal places of suffering and filth. I knew too much about Cambodia to be *sabay*. Way too much.

At the hotel, I asked my best student to stay with me. She arranged a taxi, and I was home in the Hun Sen Compound apartment within ten minutes. I crawled up the metal spiral staircase, and got on the living room floor, cool tile on my back. I pulled a large cushion from the couch, elevated my legs, and called my British doctor, using my cell phone. Without it, I would've taken a few aspirin, which would have thinned my blood, and died.

Doctor Scott arrived quickly and asked me a few questions. He pressed deeply into my lower abdomen and quickly released—the "rebound" test. I gasped with pain.

He had the boldly direct bedside manner of most doctors.

"Ah," he said. "You're bleeding internally. Appendicitis, or-- is there a chance you could be pregnant?"

Yes. We'd been trying to have a baby for six months, since he'd said he was ready. Apparently I got pregnant in March of 1997.

This was an ectopic pregnancy.

Doctor Scott said to get to the Aurora Clinic fast. He'd keep his phone turned on, he said. He dashed off to help another sick person. Clinique Aurore was right down the street. Polly came to the living room and insisted on going with me. I gingerly walked down the spiral staircase and got on a motorcycle taxi. Later I realized it was dangerous owing to the bumps in the road, but it took time to get a car taxi. Time I didn't have.

When we arrived at Clinique Aurore the doors were locked, and Cambodian medical personnel sat under an awning eating rice and fish. The pain getting off the motorcycle was horrible. I walked slowly, begging for help. Polly backed me up.

"Please, she is bleeding. She could die. Please help us!" Polly told them a Western doctor would be there soon, but I needed an ultrasound.

The staff jumped up, running to the door. Polly helped me walk, telling me not to worry, not to worry, not to worry. Workers ushered me into a tiny room. The room was small and dusty, but big enough for ultrasound technician, the Polly, and me. I sat on a gurney-type bed, and Polly helped me lie down. "Oh, Debra. Very white. No color in your face."

The ultrasound technician put gel on my abdomen and began moving the wand around. I saw her frown, and she spoke.

"Pregnancy ectopique. A liter of blood lost, and it's as high as the liver. We must cut. No time to waste. If no surgery, you will die." I became coldly logical. I couldn't die and leave my parents behind. I didn't want to die, but neither did I want HIV or Hepatitis C.

"Polly, get Ken. No transfusion. I wait."

Off Polly went to fetch Ken. She rushed out after squeezing my hand hard, and saying, "Oh, Debra," her voice low and worried. Ken didn't know anything about my situation. He had been up until probably 3 or 4 a.m. the night before, working on the *Sihanoukville*

Visitors Guide. I'd badgered him for weeks to finish it, and he couldn't move beyond the editing process and put the damn thing to bed. Clients I'd sold ads to called me every day. They pressured me. I pressured him.

Ken never woke up well. When we were first together in 1989, I slipped under the sheets with him one night and he woke up yelling, furious that I'd disturbed his sleep. He arose to drink Mountain Dew and I learned not to talk with him for the first thirty minutes. It's who he was, and I loved him despite his morning grouchiness.

I should have woken Ken when Dr. Scott said I was hemorrhaging, but I wasn't thinking clearly. My logic was to let him sleep. He'd worked so late. Yet, I was in trouble. My torso was so seized up I couldn't stand up straight. Unbeknownst to me, I'd lost more than twenty percent of my blood. My hands felt cold. I quieted myself and focused on slow, deep breaths. I wanted to survive.

When Ken appeared with Polly, he said, "What's happening?"

"Ken, I need a surgery fast. It's an ectopic pregnancy." He was wide awake now.

"What's that? Explain."

"Baby's in the tube, tube ruptured. I'm bleeding out. Get Doctor Scott. Put it together for me. I can't get a transfusion. They're not monitoring blood for HIV or Hep C, and I don't want to risk it. This kind of miscarriage is the main cause for first-trimester deaths for women. I'm in trouble." I licked my lips. I felt dry, like someone had put a tap in my foot and opened a spigot. How fast was I bleeding? My hands were icy. I stayed as still as a stone.

Ken had always been good with emergency situations. He studied medicine out of a *Merck Manual*, although in Cambodia we used *Where There is No Doctor.* Ken wasn't a natural at care providing, but in an emergency, no one did better. He stayed by my side day and night. The Khmer staff insisted I have a blood transfusion and immediately go into surgery, swarming around and muttering about my imminent death. I was dizzy and weak but lay still, waiting.

I agreed to some saline solution, and it dripped into me. I turned on my side in fetal position, protecting my abdomen. I relaxed and breathed. In slowly. Out slowly. I stopped talking. I slowed myself down.

Ken called Dr. Scott, who assembled a surgical team, including the doctor of the prime minister, a well-trained and capable surgeon. Within twenty minutes, the team arrived at the clinic, Dr. Scott, the surgeon, an anesthesiologist, and a nurse. They introduced themselves, and the diminutive surgeon assured me he'd studied in France and would take excellent care of me. I was confident in them. Then, they put me on a stretcher. At this point, my heart raced. The surgeon told Ken, "We go to surgery now. She has big problem, and we can not wait. We must proceed quickly."

Ken looked at me, and said, "It's going to be okay. I love you." Then I lost focus, and saw very little except for the sides of walls. They carried me. People stepped aside. I breathed slowly. Would I live? Would I die? I felt absolutely helpless.

I was carried to the base of a small, narrow stairway. Stairs in Cambodia are steep. I begged to be allowed to walk up the stairs. The thought of being packed up terrified me. Dr. Scott walked behind the stretcher and held my hand, reassuring me, "I'm right here. Just hold on and we'll be there." He must have been right behind someone on the end of the gurney. Tears rolled. I'd held it together for so long. I took care not to sob. I protected my body.

In the surgical room, a large dusty space with furniture here and there, I saw myself reflected in a glass cabinet door. The medical staff draped me. I avoided looking at the disturbing reflection. The team worked quickly, and their manner gave me confidence.

"Now, we turn your body," said the surgeon. I felt a needle in my back. The saddle block anesthesia eliminated all pain, but I was conscious. The surgeon talked quietly in Khmer as the team worked, only a word here and there.

At one point during the procedure, I asked if I could see Ken. He came to a door behind my head, and I looked backward at him.

He spoke quietly to me. I wanted him to know I was okay. I needed to know he was there.

"Ken, our baby is gone."

"You're going to be fine."

"But our baby."

"Are you in pain?"

"No. I'm okay. No pain."

"I love you. Hang in there."

The surgeon said, "Enough." The surgeon muttered quietly to the anesthesiologist. They probably didn't want to deal with my fear of being packed down those steep stairs. Everything got foggy, the room, the cabinet.

I woke up in a small room. To my right was a wall, a powdery cement surface with rust-colored splatters. I silently vowed to avoid it, but this was the wall I later slapped when the anesthesia wore off. This was the wall I cooled my hand on, to hold to my face.

The surgeon showed us our baby. I struggled to hold my head up. He was tiny, bent in a semicircle. Ken said, "Okay, that's enough," pushing the tray away, but I said, "Wait, wait," to look. I wanted time with my baby. The surgeon walked away holding the three-month baby in the plastic try. I fell unconscious.

Within about two hours, I woke up in the worst pain of my life from the laparotomy. My abdomen was sliced open so the surgeon could get in fast. When the anesthesia wore off, I began wailing, a quiet, strange cry that I scarcely recognized.

I begged for pain medication, and the nurse injected paracetamol into my arm. When he told me I was getting over-the-counter medicine, I was furious. I became a frightened animal, suffering and unable to escape. I was trapped in this damn clinic with dirty walls and inadequate pain management. I was torn apart, my torso an unfamiliar continent, bombed and tortured. I couldn't move. I wanted to die, to be burned up in a pyre. I couldn't live with this pain. I slapped the wall, moaning.

Ken paced around the room. He called Dr. Scott, who arrived within ten minutes. Dr. Scott and Ken understood the politics. They were diplomatic to the surgeon, who explained, "Often the Western patient becomes *addict*." The pain was so intense I wanted to die. I remember the surgeon looking irritated and explaining, "The patient can be very difficult in the first twenty-four hours." What he meant was the pain was difficult for the patient to endure. I wanted to die.

I slapped the dusty, rust-splattered wall with my hand. As a woman who had lived in Southeast Asia for several years, I hadn't gotten addicted to anything. Not heroin, not alcohol, not opium— and these things were abundant and easy to come by. I could smoke a cigarette here and there without feeling the need to use nicotine habitually. I'm just one of those rare individuals who can get away with a bit of substance abuse without selling my soul.

I was in pain, needed drugs, and needed them now.

After compliments to the surgeon, all done in the most conciliatory manner by Ken and Doctor Scott, the surgeon said that if Ken went to the pharmacy and got morphine, he would sign for it to be administered. He was frosty, puzzled that pain management should be such a consideration. He agreed to continue to be my surgeon of record, and Ken flew out the door. It took twenty minutes for him fly off on his motorcycle, make the purchase, and ride back. I will be forever thankful for morphine.

Later that night, when I got the second dose of medication, the nurse administered morphine and valium concurrently. I seemed to immediately vacate residence in my body. Ken and Malgosia thought I'd died. I woke up being tapped hard on the cheek by Malgosia. As my eyes opened, her concerned face was directly in front of mine, and she said, "Deb! Debra! Deb-o-*rah!* You *must* open your eyes and speak with us!" I stared at her, completely out of it. No pain. It was perfect. I was so completely out of it.

She and Ken stood around saying, "Oh, thank God," and I floated away, falling asleep listening to them talking about politics in the streets. In Phnom Penh, the various embassies were sharing maps and information with their nationals working in Cambodia. I was a U.S. Embassy warden, and had a list of names I needed to check in on. Remember, talking about politics with Cambodians was culturally wrong, and off limits. We westerners constantly talked about them. It was a matter of security.

The next day or so, Ken posted a map on my hospital wall that showed locations of politicians' homes. He'd gotten it from either the Australian or the U.S. Embassy. I mentioned the list of U.S. citizens to Ken. He'd pulled it out of the file, and it was on the desk at home. I fell asleep most nights listening to hushed political discussions between Malgosia and Ken.

I spent several days in the clinic recovering. In 1997, the clinic was considered good by Cambodian standards, but by Western standards, it was bleak. The walls were dirty and the narrow hospital bed was uncomfortable. The staff was reliable and courteous, and they took good care of me, although family was expected to do the majority of care providing. That's how it works in Cambodia, and for that matter, in the U.S. Anyone who thinks differently is wrong.

After that first horrible twenty-four hours, visitors brought flowers, perfumes, lotions, books, magazines, and even a television with stack upon stack of VHS videos. The administrator and director from ACE Phnom Penh went above and beyond in supporting me. Teachers and friends visited until I got tired, then tiptoed out. One day, I joked we'd have an ACE department meeting the following day at 2:00 p.m., and the work staff showed up with clipboards, ready to meet. They were so kind.

Ken and Malgosia rarely left. Ken was there unless he was at an embassy security briefing or taking care of things at home. Polly visited, pulling back my covers and checking me over thoroughly. Then she washed me down and gave me sips of winter melon tea.

On my fourth day, I lay on my hospital bed watching the movie *Kama Sutra*. It was all about sex and seduction. The movie was distracting, just what I needed. My pain was now under good control. A young male Cambodian nurse came in to inject paracetamol, which was fine now that my pain was manageable. In one scene, an amazingly beautiful East Indian servant has been chosen for sex by the king. The woman's breathing, kneeling position, and seductive eyes all make for one hot scene. My arm started burning as the male nurse—eyes glued to the screen—was injecting faster and faster. I couldn't help but laugh, but told him to slow down.

Ken slept on the floor on a small mattress. When I woke up and murmured or moaned in pain, he leaned in close, "What do you need? Tell me." When I cried quietly, he reassured me, "Let's get you well. You're going to be okay." He wouldn't talk about the baby.

"We kept you alive. That's all that matters," he said.

One day, Malgosia sat at the side of my bed and said, "You can't get pregnant again. You just *can't* do this."

Now that I wasn't consumed with pain, I had time to think about losing the baby. I was miserable, and tried to hide it from most who visited. I rolled onto my right side and faced the wall. I didn't have the heart to talk about it. I hadn't even discussed losing the baby with Ken. In fact, he never talked about it with me, not once. This made me feel very alone, as if nothing had happened.

Nothing to be sad about. Nothing at all. Maybe talking about losing the baby was upsetting to him. It's hard to know because he wouldn't talk about it. Or maybe he thought there was something wrong with me, now that I couldn't have kids. I thought he'd made me wait too long. I couldn't help but think about our perfectly fine pregnancy six years earlier. I suffered horribly thinking about all this, on my own.

As I lay in the hospital, the political situation in Phnom Penh deteriorated. Ken kept me shielded from the politics, but he was worried and I could tell. He left my room to go outside and smoke, pacing the street and watching the bakery outside. The bakers stripped off their shirts in the warmth of the ovens, and bugs flew frenetically around the fluorescent lights. Hundreds of baguettes were baked. Into the oven went the long, white dough, and workers pulled them out and put them in baskets.

Little boys wearing the baskets on their bodies walked the streets singing, "Ah, num pahn, num pahn!" In musical notes, the call fluttered between C and D, ending "pahn" on C note. This was one of the magical sounds of the street. Ken showed me this bakery later when I recovered. Baguettes in Cambodia were always riddled with bugs, small and large. You either had to look closely, or don't look at all and just eat the bugs.

A day or two before I left Polyclinique Aurore, Polly came to see me. She checked me from head to toe, scrutinizing every IV bruise, the catheter placement, and my scar. She had the thoroughness of a nurse. I always got the truth from Polly, good or bad, so I trusted her.

"How do I look?" I asked.

"A long cut, ten centimeters. Not straight, but it's okay. Don't worry. Debra, war is coming soon. Fighting, very noisy. Don't leave your house. No problem for foreigners, but don't go outside."

Our house had thick concrete walls, and I knew hers did too. Polly reassured me that her family would be fine. If things got too bad, they'd leave Phnom Penh.

"We've been through Khmer Rouge, don't worry about us!' she said. I reassured her we had lots of medicine and food. She hugged me, and left. Ken walked her out and pressed money into her hand. I'd been in the hospital for several days and was released on the 4th of July.

19

*O*ut of the Frying Pan

When I was released from the hospital, I crawled up the narrow spiral staircase to our apartment. I couldn't walk upright with the stitches across my abdomen, and felt dizzy and weak from the surgery. The building we lived in was large, and the ground floor housed the owners. We had roof access, with a steel staircase that led to the top. A sheet metal roof covered an area up there, and the view of the city was excellent, really high and unobstructed.

Another couple, young attorneys from New York doing volunteer work, had recently moved into the apartment above ours. They told us they were doing volunteer work, and would be in Cambodia for six months. The walls and the floors were so thick we couldn't hear them walking above us. Even so, four months earlier I'd heard the explosion from Sam Rainsy's rally when the grenades went off, killing so many people. That spoke to the proximity of the park to our apartment.

On July 5th, Reasey, a loyal student from The American School, came to visit. He brought a huge bag of longan berries, a deliciously sweet fruit inside a woodsy shell. Ken and I could eat a kilo of them in one sitting. Reasey had ridden his motorcycle through the groups of military police clustering the streets to warn me that bombing had started at the airport. He told me this in a quiet voice. I called Ken to come hear the news. We urged Reasey to go home. He'd sent his young family out to the countryside, but his plan was to stay in Phnom Penh and protect his home.

Ken was out the door fast. For a few months, we'd kept our pantry stocked in preparation for conflict, but while I was in the hospital we lapsed. I wasn't eating much, but I was on heavy-duty antibiotics for the surgery several times a day. The stitches in my lower abdomen kept me slightly bent at the hips. I could barely walk. Even so, I didn't feel depressed now. I was exhilarated and trying to assess the situation at hand. Were we safe here? Polly and Reasey thought so. How could we know for sure?

Lucky Supermarket, right down the street, was where most expats shopped. It was a large, western-style supermarket that carried lots of food foreigners liked, although it was expensive. When Ken got there he encountered a packed store full of people scrambling to prepare for war. He bought vegetables, bananas, yellow noodles, rice, meat, cheese, bread, eggs, Toblerone, whiskey, clove cigarettes and Marlboros. Cigarettes came in handy for sharing with soldiers. He purchased several gallons of water, along with extra antibiotics and pain reliever at the pharmacy. He took care of us very well.

He had to hire a second cyclo to bring everything, riding next to it to keep an eye so things wouldn't get stolen. He prepared us for at least two weeks. While the water in Cambodia was not potable, we could have boiled water on the gas-powered range, but relying on gas and power was not a good idea. I was nervous and excited with the knowledge they were bombing the airport area. I worried about Malgosia, who we were now such close friends with.

"Ken, try calling her again." We only had one cell phone back then.

"I just did. Not answering. Her wooden house isn't great."

"If we could reach her, we could maybe try to get her here."

"I don't know. It's pretty late in the game. Military police are crawling all over the streets." At the end of our Hun Sen Compound driveway, there was a cluster of half a dozen of them. They weren't sleeping stretched out on their motorcycles, either. They were standing up, all business.

I felt ill worrying about Malgosia. While our sturdy and elevated house had thick cement walls, she lived in a small wooden dwelling. Bullets could get through her walls easily. I couldn't bear the thought of going through a battle without her safely tucked in with us.

Suddenly, we heard a commotion outside. Ken looked out the door and laughed. He had a happy voice when he was excited, and most especially when he had news that would please me.

"Looks like your wish has come true. Oh, look! She's charming them!" He opened the curtain, and we looked out.

We watched as Malgosia, straddling her big dirt bike, sat negotiating with Hun Sen's military police. At least four of them were at the end of the compound with their machine guns surrounding her. She laughed and opened her bags to show them the contents. Her smile, tight jeans, and long legs were attracting attention. The MP's laughed with her, and they waved her in.

"Oh, my darlings, I couldn't go through it all alone! Oh, my-- it is looking very serious out there! Mr. Ken, you must tell me everything that you know!" As she talked she put her bags on the floor and wiped her forehead with her palms. It was hot, and she had taken a fast ride from the south end of Phnom Penh.

She spoke quickly, pulling items from her bag, "The police and military are everywhere, and things are all locked up. I am hearing some bombing, and it's all starting to happen. I brought things for us, Debra!" She looked at me with concern, "My love, you must be so exhausted." In fact, I couldn't have been happier. Ken and I loved Malgosia.

And in her bags? Evian facial hydrating spray, lemons, butter, and eggs to cook hollandaise sauce. Clothing and her passport. Her thick pink jade necklace was on a gold chain around her neck. She pulled several damp one-hundred dollar bills out of her bra. Nearly immediately, we heard her phone go off, and as she was in the bathroom washing off the dirt from her fast motorcycle ride, I answered it. Malgosia had taught me how to say "yes" in Polish, so I said, "Tak, Tak" waiting for Malgosia to reappear. Her mother was worried. Having fled Poland to move the family to Canada, she understood political upheaval.

July 5th, 1997 began the three-day "factional fighting" of Cambodia. We called it the coup. Everyone did. Although I was in pain from surgery and could barely walk, I trudged up the stairs outside our apartment to watch street battle from the rooftop canopy. We were torn between the rooftop and watching the action, and staying inside where it was safe. We went back and forth, as it was hard to stop watching. From the roof, we saw smoke billow from the southwest side of town in a huge column.

Hun Sen's soldiers sat on rooftops around us, with mounted machine guns. We smiled and waved at them, but did not want them to be distracted. I remember a handsome soldier grinning and mouthing *Ot Bahnha* (no problem), and then looking back through his sights on his machine gun, set on a spotting scope. No problem, foreigners.

At one point, we heard and then saw, a tank roll along the street from the south. Captured men marched in their underwear with their hands cuffed behind their backs. Ken wrote about one captured soldier:

God knows what happened to the poor guy. A lot of guys in his position never made it out. Some of Ranariddh's body guards (and others) turned up later in shallow graves with their eyes gouged out. Many Khmers believe that the last sight a man sees before death is frozen on the back of his eyes. Hence, to prevent the murderers identity from being discovered, the eyes are gouged out. Human rights people are crying "torture," but I'm afraid it's just straightforward murder and maybe even the fortunes of war, Khmer-style (though if it ever comes my turn I think I'll take my eye-gouging after being killed, thank you).

Ken, Malgosia and I went inside right after we saw the tank, worried for the captured soldiers. This wasn't a game, and we knew that they would be killed, no doubt. Bombing intensified, and tremors and explosions rocked our home. At one point, the landlords, who lived on the ground floor, came upstairs and asked us to come down. The cheerful landlord explained he had a good place. His wife was sweeping out a bomb shelter just outside of the house. She waved and smiled. Even in the face of danger, they were cheerful. They said if it got worse, we should all go in. We thanked them and went back upstairs to our place.

The bombing was so close it shook the building. I panicked, trying to crawl underneath our bed. Ken yelled at me, "What the hell are you doing?" He was unnerved to see me that afraid. We were on the phone nonstop to citizens on my U.S.

Embassy Warden call list, and several people called us for news, as we were in the thick of things, between the Independence Monument and the Tonle Sap River.

Fighting was worse in the Tuol Kork area and near Wat Phnom, as I recall. An Australian teacher we worked with was reportedly in a wooden house near Wat Phnom in the thick of gunfire, and was lying down in a bathtub to avoid the bullets coming through the walls. She was terrified and talking on a cellphone with low battery. When it was all over, she left her job in Phnom Penh and sued for the remainder of her teaching contract. She wanted out of Cambodia.

At dinnertime, I asked Ken to go upstairs and invite the young attorneys upstairs to eat with us. He didn't want to. He was afraid we'd run out of supplies. For all we knew, we could be trapped inside for days. I made the case for sharing, which was usually his inclination. Because I was in such a weak condition, he was especially protective of our food stores. Finally, he went upstairs to invite them.

When they came downstairs to join us, she admitted they had nothing but bottled water upstairs. It was obvious she blamed her husband, and I felt sorry for him. She should have seen the writing on the wall, too. The staples holding my abdomen together were unforgiving and uncomfortable, and if Ken had insisted we not share, I wouldn't have pushed it. In hindsight, we did the right thing.

Our meal, stir-fried noodles with little bits of pork and vegetables, was impossible for the couple to eat, as they were Jewish, which they disclosed after I cooked, so I made more pasta and vegetables. Ken stared at me as though I'd gone crazy. I told the attorneys we'd eat the leftovers, and it was no trouble at all.

After dinner, we went up to the rooftop again to watch the red tracers in the night sky. It had been a long day, and the CPP (Hun Sen's party) and FUNCINPEC (Prince Ranariddh's party) soldiers were still at it. We felt safer than we had earlier in the day, when the bombing around our area was so intense. We went to bed, and hoped for a better July 6th. While fighting continued, it had calmed down in the Hun Sen Compound, where our apartment was situated.

The next day, we still heard gunfire, but the fighting wasn't as

noisy. Apparently, the CPP—2nd Prime Minister Hun Sen's side—
had won the battle. At this point, we heard that CPP soldiers were
openly looting in the streets. Our friend was killed by Hun Sen's
military police, which was the worst news of all. Michael Senior was a
friend who taught at ACE school. He was adopted as a baby during
the early Khmer Rouge years by Canadian parents, but he chose to
return to his native country. He was a well-loved teacher at ACE
school, as well as a journalist.

I met him when I lived in Sihanoukville. I was riding my
motorcycle back to town from Sokha Beach, and before getting to
the Golden Lion Roundabout I saw a Cambodian guy and girl
walking along. I stopped and spoke to them, in Khmer. The guy
looked at me and nodded and smiled. Later, I met him in town at a
pub, and he came up to me laughing, and asked if I spoke English. It
was Michael Senior.

"I didn't know what you were saying earlier," he said. "No idea!"

Michael was a handsome young adult, happy in Cambodia,
making relationships and well liked by everyone. He got lots of
opportunities in Cambodia, with good looks, a friendly personality,
and a personable way about him. He got married and had a baby.
Time passed.

On July 7th, he took his camera out onto the street to take
photographs of the looting. His wife and brother-in-law were with
him. One of the CPP looters screamed at him in Khmer to stop, and
shot him in the knee. His language skills weren't great, but he
apologized, "Som toe, som toe." Sorry. Sorry. The looter shot him
dead, in front of his wife and his brother-in-law. Our friends Marie
Claude and Raaj were heartbroken. They were close friends with him.
Michael's wife went to Raaj's house, crying and upset.

Raaj drove to a pagoda where corpses had been taken in carts,
holding a white "surrender" flag out the car window the whole way.
It was a tremendous risk, but that's how friends were in Phnom
Penh. Officials gave soldiers instructions to immediately cremate the
bodies, destroying evidence. Raaj looked for Michael, who was
stacked with several other bodies awaiting cremation. It was so hard

on him. He not only lost his friend, but had to see it all. We all felt so sad. I hated the soldiers for killing Michael.

On the 7th, things calmed down considerably. Malgosia and Ken went for a ride around the city on her motorcycle. Several of the other foreigners were riding motorcycles around too. My body ached. The activities of the last few days, along with the stress, had not done me any favors. My emotional pain at losing the baby was tremendous, but I was so distracted with the military conflict I didn't have time to think much about it.

I knew I should be resting. With Ken out riding around the war zone with Malgosia, I was nervous. Only two fit on the motorcycle, but I couldn't have gone anyway. I could barely walk. I gathered up laundry to hand wash. I always cooked or cleaned when under stress. Polly was safely tucked into her family home near P'sar Thmei, and I was glad for it. Maybe it was time to get out of Cambodia. I wondered what our next move would be.

As I held a heavy, wet towel to let the water drip, I felt sharp pain. It radiated through my abdomen. I sat down and used both hands to wring the towel, letting the cold tile support the weight of it. I held the wet towel on my face and felt its coolness. I was tired, so tired. Where were they?

An hour or so later, Ken and Malgosia got back. They'd seen quite a lot. Looting was still going on. They'd gone up and down the riverfront, and just around town. Ken was exuberant they hadn't seen any problems on the streets, and over the next several days sat at the riverfront cafes and railed about *Voice of America's* declarations that there was violence at *that very moment* on the streets of Phnom Penh.

He was furious the media was so eager to bash Cambodia, and to be honest, most of us were tired of the allusions to the Khmer Rouge years. Cambodia had more contemporary problems to address. For one, the grenade attack in March that killed sugarcane sellers and other innocent people trying to make a living, as well as Sam Rainsy's bodyguard, who threw himself on top of Rainsy after the first explosion. Now, the coup had put Cambodia right in the crosshairs of the international donor community.

20

*U*SAID and a Calico Cat

Back then every westerner in Phnom Penh called what happened on July 5th, 6th, and 7th "the coup." The second week of July, someone was selling t shirts that said "Democracy? *Hun*believable…*Sen*sational. They were worn all over town.

Although all the people I knew called it a coup, Hun Sen was the second prime minister, and violently seizing power that you already possess is not a coup. The phrase "factional fighting" might be fair, and First Prime Minister Prince Ranariddh was alleged to be consorting with the Khmer Rouge up north, rallying them to join "his side." Anyway, both prime ministers had their own armies. Second Prime Minister Hun Sen's army won. First Prime Minister Prince Ranariddh scooted out of Cambodia, although he returned in March 1998 and filled a different political position. There has been only one prime minister in Cambodia for decades—Prime Minister Hun Sen. Those who live in Cambodia now and wish to be more politically correct call it "factional fighting." If you lived in Phnom Penh that particular weekend, it was a coup.

When the fighting was finished, Ken and I went to the printers and paid the print shop owner the balance for our first tourist magazine to Cambodia, *The Sihanoukville Visitors Guide*. We owed $2,000.00 to the printer, and we were determined to pay it. He was delighted to see us, and surprised. So many foreigners had fled. He thought he was going to lose money, and we felt good about paying him. We hoped the customers who had paid for 50% of the advertisements felt as good about paying their balances due to us.

If we'd left, it would have destroyed our reputations. All those advertisers would have paid for ads they didn't receive. We weren't going to do that. More than that, we weren't going to do that to *them*. The Khmer people had suffered enough. Over the course of the next few months, young expats in Cambodia patted themselves on the back for staying, while the NGO types (the non-governmental agency people, including USAID) fled in droves. Actually, the majority of foreigners working in Phnom Penh left. Not us. I would have left, but Ken didn't want to. The ectopic pregnancy was causing me a lot of pain. I'd overdone it after the surgery. I took ibuprofen and just kept moving. Ken was resolute about staying. I brought it up more than once.

"I'm in pain constantly, Ken."

"You're going to need to give yourself some time to heal."

I said, "Let's get this guide finished, and get out of here."

"I'm not leaving. The Cambodian people need us now more than ever, don't you think? We need money either way. We need to keep working," he said. I couldn't argue with him. I was so exhausted from the surgery. When I brought up leaving, he ranted that it would be throwing our business away. He wasn't happy. His plan to keep me busy with a baby wasn't going well, I thought.

Ken decided to move us out of the Hun Sen Compound before possible retaliation. Hun Sen had won the first round July 5th, but we couldn't predict there wouldn't be more fighting at some point. It was like anticipatory grief, that fear that someone you love is going to die, but instead it was constant fear about more military battles. Ken was out one night. He said at the Irish Bar, but he was probably at Martini's or Sharkey's. They were the bars in town with lots of prostitutes. He met Shawn, an American who worked for USAID. Shawn worked in Phnom Penh. His wife and two children from the USA were living in Phnom Penh with him, in a large villa in the Tuol Kork area. His salary was high, and all his living expenses were paid for. He got a per diem for food, and USAID was paying for security guards and maids, too. His superiors with USAID told him he had to leave for a few months. USAID was withdrawing financial support from Cambodia.

Shawn asked Ken if we'd live in his villa for free while he was gone. The condition was that we were to keep an eye on his place and keep it from being looted. He'd be gone for three months, perhaps longer. When Ken told me about it, I was glad for an interim place to live, so we'd have time to find our own new apartment or home in Phnom Penh. We visited the fellow at his villa, and it was huge and beautifully decorated. In an outside office, I saw an old walnut desk, and realized it must weigh at least a few hundred pounds. Shawn explained it was his childhood desk, shipped from the USA in a huge cargo container.

"Wow, are you just going to leave it here?"

"No," he replied. "Of course not. I just didn't want to pay for a storage unit in the U.S., so I had all my stuff shipped here. When we go back home, we'll have it shipped back with everything else."

"And USAID paid for that?" I asked.

"Oh, they pay for everything," he conceded. Ken and I looked each other and rolled our eyes when Shawn turned his back to us, continuing with the tour. He showed us around his villa with its large, grandiose upstairs. His bookshelves included at least two hundred books, all from his home in the U.S. I was puzzled that an aid agency to help the poor people of Cambodia was paying so much to ship heavy books and the boyhood desk to Phnom Penh. He pointed out one bedroom after another.

We told Shawn we had Cambodian workers, and they depended on us for food and money. We weren't willing to lay them off. They were like family to us at that point. We provided them food and lodging, not because we needed ongoing guard and maid services, but because they were good people and had asked us for jobs. Ken's motodop was Mr. Lim from Prey Veng. He hadn't gone to school at all in his life, but had amassed a good amount of money while driving UNTAC workers around on a motorcycle, which he'd borrowed from a friend. He was then able to buy his own motorcycle with the generous UNTAC salary. We were impressed with his motivation to earn money for his family.

When we went to the U.S. for a few months in 1996, we returned to find Mr. Lim blind in one eye. A fake doctor gave him two red pills, two blue pills, and some Tiger Balm—the typical prescription from a doctor in Cambodia. We were devastated for him. Polly had a family to take care of as well, and we wanted to look out for her. Shawn agreed that would be fine for our workers to come to Tuol Kork.

After a month of living at the huge villa in Tuol Kork, it was clear that Shawn's security staff wanted us out. When USAID staff had been evacuated to the U.S.A., other Khmer security guards were looting furniture and items the USAID staff left behind, and Shawn's guards wanted to do the same. There is a carpetbagger mentality following war, and we, along with our staff, were interfering with the natural order of things. Shawn's staff began harassing us.

I tutored a few children, including Polly's daughter (who had lived with us for three years at this point) and Polly's niece. Srey Mum, a bright little girl, filled such a void in my heart. I loved her, and watched her comings and goings, although her mom was her true guardian. I was Ma ti pi, Mom number two.

Now, I could hear Srey Mum's timid voice calling. The security guard was out there. Why wasn't he opening the gate? After the gunfire in the streets, I was quick to flare and very defensive of Srey Mum and her cousin.

Srey Mum called, "Ma! Ma! Help!" I was terrified that she was getting hurt or kidnapped. Those were frightening times in Phnom Penh.

When I went outside, the stern-faced guard told me Mr. Shawn refused to allow any "outsiders" in except Ken and me. I called Ken out of the house, and explained the guard refused to let in the two children.

"You will open the gate immediately," Ken told the guard. The guard, immobile, repeated his American boss's orders. Right then and there, Ken phoned Shawn to ask what was going on, despite the time difference. It was midnight on the east coast of the U.S.A.

Shawn said the guards claimed we were running an English school, and he didn't want his home to be turned into a school.

Ken said, "Two children? Two ten-year-olds?"

Shawn deferred, but he was irritated. He said the guard was calling him with reports every day. Shawn asked for the phone to be handed to the guard. The guard, hearing Shawn's order, opened the gate, staring at the children. The little girls entered, looking scared. When Ken got the phone back, Shawn said the guards had concerns about the number of people coming and going, and he wasn't sure whether to believe the guards or us.

That night, Ken and I talked. All the time we'd been there, the guards stared sullenly at us, and wrote our comings and goings in a log. Not only that, but our staff members had disclosed they were afraid of the workers at the Tuol Kork compound. They said Shawn's workers told them to go away, and stay away.

This infuriated us, and we decided to leave immediately. This would open Shawn's home to the same looting to which the other aid workers' homes were being subjected, but we no longer cared. Let the giant desk disappear. Let the wife's books about the jade gate and three-day cleanses be taken. Let the expensive mahogany furniture, purchased with USAID dollars, be carted off on cyclos. Ken and I crafted a letter to Shawn:

Dear Shawn,

Thank you for the opportunity to stay in your villa. We will be here for five additional days, so you have time to travel back to Phnom Penh from the USA. We have decided, as a result of the recent problems with you and your security staff, to move immediately. While we agreed to protect your belongings in exchange for rent, it has become clear that you are actually now protecting your villa from us. This is offensive beyond measure. Your security staff will be in charge of your belongings within approximately five days. We will photograph your home as we leave, and your guards will—of course—log our exit time and date for you in the journal at the entry gate. When we depart in five days, we will leave the keys with the guard. I am disappointed that you would criticize my wife for teaching a few Cambodian children English language skills. We both see hypocrisy in your hesitation to have a few Khmer children at the dining room table in this three thousand square foot villa—paid for by American dollars.

Ken and Debra

Within the week, we were out of there, and glad to be. The security guards gloated as we left, waving goodbye. Polly found us a villa on Street 232 near Olympic Stadium. The rent was $600.00 per month, and we paid for it out of money we earned teaching, observing elections, or our business Canby Publications, Ltd. Since Polly had found the villa, she got a kickback from the owner, and perhaps a monthly gratuity. That's how things worked in Phnom Penh.

It was probably 3,000 square feet, not like the place in Tuol Kork, but large enough so that Polly and Mr. Lim, Ken's motodop who was now our security guard (with one eye, his driving had gotten unsafe), could have accommodations. Polly had a separate kitchen, and could use *prahok*, the smelly fish sauce, to her heart's content. Her family was always in and out of there visiting. It was a happy place for all of us.

During that time, we acquired a cat of three colors—*ch'ma pua bi*. A calico was considered good luck. When Srey Mum brought home the white cat with dramatic orange and black splotches, we were skeptical. Cats just didn't fare well in Cambodia, nor did dogs. There were guys with baskets who stole them to make meals. Even now there's a dogcatcher who rides a bike around Siem Reap with an attached basket. Into the basket goes the catch of the day, anything from a fat tabby cat to a tiny dog.

Our Cambodian daughter, Srey Mum was probably eleven years old now. We sent her to Chinese school and English school. Polly encouraged Srey Mum to call us "Pa and Ma ti pi," and Srey Mum usually just called me "Mom." She was a natural at her studies, and learned English rapidly. It was with great excitement that she brought home the lucky cat.

We worried. We'd already had problems with one four-year-old Chinese kid in our gated compound in Sihanoukville. He drowned every kitten and cat he could lay his hands on, despite our conversations with his mother. We'd look out our apartment window to see him plodding toward the cistern with an unsuspecting kitten.

Sometimes, we beat him to the well--"No, no! put kitty *down*, Dara!"—but there were times when we could not. This upset me. We got a small tabby while we lived in Sihanoukville, but it disappeared, and I suspect it went the way of the cistern. Polly shielded me from bad news, and I remember her cheery laugh, "I don't know, Deb."

Srey Mum talked us into keeping the calico cat. Mandu emerged as a loving pet. She sat on our desks and beds with her white paws tucked under her body. When Polly met with a new neighbor, she would walk down the street with our cat, so Mandu's presence could bless the home with her luck. Everyone in the home loved her.

Everything happy in Cambodia seemed to end tragically for us. Mandu died at the hands of a bad vet. He did a mucked-up spay job on her, and when I called him back to our home after hours of watching her suffer and die, I queried him closely. He stared at me calmly, with the strangest amber-colored eyes.

I insisted he give me back the $40.00 Polly gave him to spay Mandu. When he said he'd have to talk to his boss, I got his boss on the phone and talked, while holding my hand out to the man with amber eyes. When I got the money back, I ripped it into shreds, like Tony at karaoke, and escorted him to the door.

And then we went to the Cat Pagoda. Yes, the *Cat Pagoda*. Cambodia was mostly Buddhist, and pagodas were sprinkled throughout Phnom Penh. Some pagodas were for praying and spending time. Pagodas also offer cremation and funeral services. This particular pagoda was loaded up with felines and elderly nuns, who took care of them. Just a few days earlier, Polly had taken Mandu's three kittens to the Cat Pagoda. Now that Mandu was gone, we needed those kittens back.

When we pulled into the pagoda, I was shocked at the huge quantity of cats. It was like a Humane Society without the spay and neuter component. There were black cats, white cats, gray cats, orange cats, small cats, tall cats, fat cats, thin cats. They lounged, reclined on the cool cement of the structures, scratched in dirt to relieve themselves, and ate from old chipped dishes and bowls. Nuns—very old women with shaved heads wearing white, long draped monk-like attire—approached us.

Adopting kittens from the Cat Pagoda was going to turn into an expensive operation. There were mouths to be fed here! The kittens needed to be shampooed! The nuns needed compensation too.

"Tomorrow come back," the nuns told us. The agreed-upon sum was $10.00 per cat, and we threw in some extra money for the good of the order. The next day, Polly picked up three kittens from the Cat Pagoda. While they looked similar to Mandu's kittens, two of them probably carried no DNA whatsoever from our cat.

Srey Mom named them. Coffee, an orange male, grew to be a twenty-pound behemoth, and the neighbors two doors down decided they couldn't live without him. He would occasionally wander back to see what we were having for dinner, but he was happy at the neighbor's house. The cat Tea died. I don't remember why. Cinnamon grew to be a large, orange tabby.

When I left Cambodia in 2001, Cinnamon the tabby cat fell into the huge square cistern on the roof and drowned. I'm glad I wasn't there, although by that time death was as familiar as my shadow.

21

$\mathcal{D}$eath Again

In Cambodia, people died so often I became numb to it. The first few deaths were upsetting. Kübler-Ross's paradigm hadn't helped me that much when I was dealing with my brother's death, although I was good at denial. In Phnom Penh, I had to force myself to send the condolence card or attend the service before moving on. I'd finally learned coping skills, and cherry-picked the grief stages that worked for me. I usually skipped the depression stage and stayed in denial. I had some lapses into anger and depression, but stayed calm and kept my head down. I got lots of practice in Cambodia.

People from the U.S. have told me over the years that life doesn't mean as much to Asian people. That's false. The people I met in Cambodia and Thailand loved their families and friends deeply, and suffered tremendously when they died. Polly grieved for her sister who died in a motorcycle accident just as I grieved for my brother. "Life is cheap over there to those people!"—is said as a statement of fact, usually by know-it-alls who have never been to Southeast Asia. It's true that in developing countries like Cambodia, fewer safeguards exist. Handrails aren't placed where they might save a life. Drunk teenagers can fall off balconies, because the tenth floor sliding glass window actually opens.

Knowledge is power when it comes to healthcare, and Cambodians in the countryside lack information about preventative medicine. It's not their fault. In the 90s, they showed up at hospitals when they were so far gone it was impossible to bring them back. I saw people bringing collapsed loved ones to hospital, so out of it they appeared deceased, wheeled in with a cyclo. Sihanouk Center of Hope Hospital in Phnom Penh, where I taught English for three months, changed lives for people in Cambodia. More than once, Ken and I sent people there: "It's free! No, it really is!" Sadly, many poor people were illiterate, so fliers and billboards went unnoticed. The word had to be spread from person to person.

Too many westerners still die in accidents in the Kingdom of Wonder, often twenty and thirty-year-olds. Foreigners with drug and alcohol issues die of heroin overdose, injecting product that hasn't been stepped on a hundred times over. Druggies get in all sorts of trouble in Cambodia. Two website communities, *Cambodia Expats Online* and *Khmer 440* report deaths in the community and sometimes include the grisly photos. The Khmer newspapers always run photos of people who die in accidents.

Police reports often attribute overdoses to fainting or "heart attack." It goes on and on. Drowns while swimming. Dies in double suicide. Crushed motorcycle under giant truck. Falls from sixth floor. Drug overdose, needle in arm. Heart attack. Heart attack. Heart attack. Drug overdose causes heart attack. Drugs in Cambodia are often fatal to recreational users. The users think that heroin is heroin the world around. No. And cocaine doesn't exist in Phnom Penh. It's a white powder, but it's not cocaine. Lots of overdoses there nowadays.

Be warned.

When Khmer people died, family members in Cambodia washed and dressed the body for display—sometimes on a mat in the front room—and they arranged cremation at a pagoda. Ken and I came to appreciate the hundred-day rice soup ritual. One hundred days after losing a loved one, family and friends came together and shared chicken soup with rice. It's the ultimate comfort food, piping hot with a rich, flavorful broth. Ken said, "A hundred days is enough time to grieve. After that, it's time to get on with living." I agreed in theory. Practice was harder. We had many occasions to eat the chicken rice soup.

Big Stan died. He was a quiet fellow in his forties who used to sit at the Angkor Arms Pub. He smoked cigarettes and chatted quietly with his girlfriend, a tall prostitute about his age. This was rare for a man in Cambodia. It was typical to see forty-year-old men with twenty-year-old women. Big Stan's life was a mystery, but he kept to himself. When I read Big Stan was dead in a hotel room, his private parts cut off and shoved down his throat, I was upset and shocked. I liked him. We all wondered if he had gotten caught up in drugs or perhaps slept with the wrong woman. The murder shocked us.

One morning, Ken and I were sleeping when we heard the sound of motorcycles pouring into our gated compound. We heard the funeral music. When someone dies in Cambodia, loud chime-like music plays. Its particular rhythm of an eighth and a dotted eighth note is deafening, and announces to people within miles around that someone has died. When foreigners wake up with that music nearby at full volume, it's best to go to a hotel for a few days, because the music is nonstop. It would be rude to interfere and ask grieving families to turn it down, as it's part of the ritual. I've heard of some people doing that. Not a good idea.

Sihanoukville in the early '90s was a small community, completely different than now. We heard the funeral music, and started to worry. Sure enough, our students buzzed in on motorcycles and knocked at our apartment door to tell us that Vanny, a gentle older student of about forty-five committed suicide. She'd lived through the terrible Khmer Rouge years, and struggled with depression. She said she was often sad. Being a wife and a mom to four children she loved deeply kept her going for years, but her depression was too great. She drank insecticide to kill herself, our students said. The news was a hard blow.

Ken struggled with depression, and I did too. I didn't realize it at the time. Ken thought he'd inherited it, and often told me when he was feeling bad. I figured I was just depressed because of my brother and other deaths. We both suffered with Vanny's death, for quite a long time.

When we arrived at Vanny's home, the crowd of people parted for us. She was lying on a bamboo mat. White, filmy gauze covered her body. Candles and incense burned. Women gestured to Ken and me to move closer. They removed the gauze. Flies buzzed around. It was hot. I felt a wave of vertigo, and knew I'd faint. I sat down and put my hands together in prayer, in the courteous fashion with legs to the side, curled behind me. To Buddhists, the feet are the lowest part of the body, and considered dirty. We'd learned to be cautious and never point them at anyone. Shoes were left outside of homes. Likewise, we never touched anyone's head, the most sacred part. Even with children, it was wrong to do that.

Ken braced my body with his legs. I stopped myself from losing consciousness, but barely. I tried to focus on anything but Vanny's body, and finally I had the strength to stand up, and we moved outside. Later we followed the funeral procession to the cemetery outside of town, and Chinese spirit money rained down from the funeral wagon.

Then, Steve died. When Ken started doing election work in Phnom Penh, he made friends with Steve. Steve had majored in political science. Ken liked him and so did I. Steve's Khmer skills were better than most, and he made sense of the tangled strands of Khmer politics and alliances. Khmer politics and legal decisions didn't follow rule of law, but were a tangle of personalities, alliances, agreements, bribes and favors owed. Steve was able to explain the quagmire of politics, and was pretty funny about it: "'person a' was jealous, so he murdered 'person b' and ended the problem, but then...."

Rumor had it that he partied hard. One night, he was singing karaoke with beer girls pouring him cold ones. People said he'd used an opiate along with alcohol, but we never found out. He collapsed and died fairly quickly. Ken and he had worked together, and given elections presentations at U.S. Embassy meetings. Ken was devastated.

Then, my friend Tim died. Tim owned a nightclub next to the Heart of Darkness, back in the days when street 51 was a more innocent place. Tim's bar was called The Duck Club, and I designed his logo, a duck wearing a beret and sunglasses. Tim loved music. He put a decent keyboard in his club, with a sound system. People brought in guitars and tambourines, and Saturday nights we jammed. I played keyboards or banged on the tambourine. I missed playing in my band back in Oregon, so it was special for me.

When Tim died in a car accident, his funeral was packed. I rarely go to funerals, but I went to his. I was furious at the driver who had run into Tim's car that I could hardly attend his service. Around that time, I realized I was also sick of living there. I didn't want to explore the country anymore. A lack of curiosity and anger usually signal depression for me. I was at a crossroads. Leaving would mean leaving Ken. I couldn't even think about it, and when it crossed my mind, I shoved it away fast.

Next, Ken's friend Arijhan died. Ken played chess with Ari, and said Ari was his best friend. Ari was a Dutch artist, a tall and lanky man with a gentle manner. He designed some art for the covers of the guides we were printing. When Ari was diagnosed with cancer, Ken spent a lot of time at his house. Like many of the guys, Ari had a young wife and one child, as I remember.

When Ari was struggling with pain, Ken asked Ari if he might want some pot from the market, and Ari held up a bag with about a quarter of an ounce, "This should be enough." He meant it was enough until the end of his life. The last week was hard, but Ken was there for it. Losing Arijahn affected Ken badly. We talked about Ari more than once.

Charly of La Paillote and Chris of Angkor Arms died, but they were older men and had health issues. Ken loved the older guys, and taught them how to use their computers. Charly and Chris both would held the mouse high up in the air, pointing it at the monitor. It made Ken laugh. Charly had emphysema, and would not stop smoking. Chris was ex-military, one of the UNTAC holdovers, and he lived in a big villa and invested in a local pub. He was diabetic, but he ignored that, shaking a glass with ice in it and calling his maid to bring him drinks and snacks. That pretty much sums things up.

Tragedy hit close to home when Polly told me her sister, Srey Nuon, was doing badly. She had struck her breast on the handlebar of a bicycle, and it was infected. This sounded odd to me. Ken and I agreed to check on Polly's sister. We got a taxi and drove to the market first. We picked up a thirty-pound bag of rice, dried fish, fresh fruit and vegetables, and some medications. We both loved Polly, and if her family needed something, we wanted to help.

We suspected Srey Nuon had cancer, so we stopped at the pharmacy and picked up morphine, valium, and some ibuprofen and stool softeners. We weren't taking any chances. In Cambodia, people let their illnesses get to the brink of death before seeing doctors. I worked with Hope International Hospital for a while, so I saw this a lot. This was the case with Srey Nuon.

When we arrived at Srey Nuon and her husband's place, it was about 90 degrees Fahrenheit. The afternoon sun had lulled everyone into a bit of a stupor, but my heart raced. The husband and kids greeted us, and were grateful for the rice and food. In fact, they were gleeful. They ushered us to the open-air hut where Srey Nuon lay in a hammock, and Polly handed me her small jar of Tiger Balm, motioning to put it under my nose. Not fast enough.

The smell of rotting flesh hit me full force, and I tried to hide my discomfort. Srey Nuon lay there, with her nine-year-old daughter fanning her. She apologized. Her breast cancer had ulcerated into the hammock. Once again, I fought fainting. The inside of my nose was burning from Tiger Bam. Srey Nuon pulled aside her shirt to show me her ravaged breast. Ken left the hut, whispering, "I can't do this." I squeezed his hand and said, "go." I cried with her and held her hand, although I was dizzy coping with the stench.

Nuon said, "I can't live, I can't live," and she cried. She took her daughter's hand and put it in mine. She was giving me her daughter. I couldn't take her child, although I thanked her. The family was large and the girl would've been desperately unhappy to leave them. Ken came back in, and we talked with Srey Nuon and her husband about pain control. She was suffering, and we gave her and her husband instructions to follow with the medications. Polly helped with translating. We left, feeling shaken.

The next day, Ken and I went to Sihanouk Hospital Center of Hope. I met with a doctor who said that based on my description, her fate was all but sealed, probably in her final days--but she could come to the hospital. The doctor said the medications we'd taken her were good choices for a person with advanced cancer. A few days later, the family got her in a car. They took her to the hospital, but nothing could be done.

Srey Nuon said the valium kept her from crying, and kept her calm. Polly delivered food and medications to the family and let us know how they were doing. Srey Nuon died in June of 1998. Not long after, her husband drank himself to death. The children all went to live with different family members. The little daughter lived with Polly's family and looked to be doing well when I saw her in 2001.

With all these deaths, I got better at dealing with loss. I ate the chicken soup after 100 days and got back to living. Even so, my conversations with Ken went like this:

"Ken, have you noticed that people are dying here all the time?"

"They're dying everywhere all the time."

"No, Ken. This is over the top. Seriously, every few months someone we know drowns, gets electrocuted, shot, or is in a car accident."

"I'm not sure it's any worse here," he said. "We're just living closer to the people." He was wrong. I was beginning to rely on him less for information. He was manipulating me, and seemed to be living in a different reality.

"Ken, what makes you so sure we're safe here? I've nearly died. The hospitals aren't that great either. Come on."

Our conversations began to keep me awake at night. We hardly grieved one person before another one was gone. I didn't want to live like this. Too much death. It made me think of my brother, and I was weary of grieving. I'd gotten better at it: practice makes perfect! But I was sick of death. Looking back, I was so naïve. I shake my head at how I was betrayed by the person I loved and trusted the most.

Back then, I was in constant pain, suffering depression and experiencing PTSD every time someone honked their car horn. And my husband was enjoying Cambodia. But why? Why couldn't he see I was unhappy? Why was he so committed to staying here?

22

Work is a Four-Letter Word

I discovered "why" soon enough. After the events of 1997, business wasn't good. Neither was our marriage. Ken started spending a lot of time with Tony, an Australian builder and contractor. Tony's girlfriend, a beautiful Vietnamese girl, had long, straight hair past her waist. Tony had building contracts around Phnom Penh, and he earned himself a notorious reputation for withholding pay from his Cambodian staff workers. Ken's role with Tony's company was bookkeeping, and Tony started pressuring him to cook the books. Ken talked about it a lot, and he stopped sleeping at night. Something else was going on, though. Ken was spending time with Tony and the taxi girls. Tony wasn't paying him, and Ken told me he was hanging out with Tony to ingratiate himself, so he'd get paid. I didn't think that was entirely true.

Ken didn't like his appearance. When he was a kid, he felt like the ugly duckling of his family. Both brothers were cute and personable, but he was plain and sulky. He said he didn't get attention from people. He said his girlfriend Sharol yelled insults at him about his looks when she was angry. I didn't ask him what she'd said, but whatever it was, it was mean. He'd told me that when he was young, he was a skinny science fiction nerd that used big words. He wore a beard to cover a "weak chin," the sign of a weak man, a family member had told him. An ex-girlfriend's mom had called him a worm, whatever that meant. It bothered him.

He was attractive, but he was thin our first few years in Cambodia. I was self-conscious about my size, too. I carried at least fifty pounds more than women in Cambodia. After I lost the first baby, I was sedentary, guarding the sharp pains in my lower abdomen, and gained weight. I was heavy for a period of time, not obese, but twenty pounds overweight. My self-esteem suffered, as western men living in Cambodia called western women "buffalos" within earshot of us women. No, I'm not kidding. One day at ACE school, a few months after losing the baby, I found a note on the stairs.

"Don't tell those big-ass administrators I'm taking Friday off."

I showed the note to my manager. We argued back and forth over who the note was about, and tried to laugh it off. Almost without exception, western women were compared unfavorably with tiny Asian women. So, Ken wished he was bigger, while I wished I was smaller.

When Tony decided he liked Ken, Ken was flattered. Tiny Vietnamese girls flocked around good-looking Tony, and next to the Asian girls, Ken was a big man. Karaoke parties were the sites of business meetings—a mix of business and pleasure. I was no longer invited. It didn't leave Ken much time to work on the travel guides, but he didn't want to sell ads, and by then, I refused to sell. After the surgeries, I couldn't ride around on a motorcycle with all the potholes and heat. So, Ken decided to apply to work as an election observer, a role he was filled well.

These were hard times for us. I didn't want to live in Cambodia anymore, and Ken wouldn't discuss leaving. I'd almost died in Cambodia, and it wasn't enough for him to leave. I had a surgery in which I had to beg for pain medications, and seeing my misery wasn't enough. Ken told everyone that my surgery was as good as I could have obtained anywhere. Easy for him to say. A military conflict on the streets of the city wouldn't shake him. My attempts to talk with him were fruitless. He stonewalled at every approach.

"Ken, things have gone south since 1997. Let's get out of here."

He stayed silent.

I pushed, "Ken, can we talk?"

"About what?" he asked.

"Leaving. Going home. Back to Oregon, Ken."

He exploded, "I won't go back to the U.S.! It's a boring place with unhappy people marching in lockstep and paying heavy taxes! I've put too much work into this business to throw it all away!"

"You're okay with cooking financial books for Tony? Are you waiting for Cambodia to become a tourist destination again? Come on, Ken. I thought you liked Oregon. Why can't we talk about it?"

"I'm not leaving. I've done too much work to throw it away," he said, staring at me. I didn't get it. What about Cambodia was keeping him here? He'd loved hiking in Oregon, exploring the snowy peaks of Mount Hood and hiking through the Three Sisters Wilderness Area. We'd hiked Eagle Cap Wilderness, and climbed Mount St. Helens. Silver Falls State Park, The Wallowa Mountains, and The Steens Mountains were our playgrounds. We weren't hiking in Cambodia. Heat. Land mines. And aside from those elements, I was so tired of living there. I'd lost my curiosity. I was depressed.

In part, I blamed Ken's personality change on Tony, who was throwing around Australian aid dollars and partying with taxi girls. Tony was a bad influence, and Ken was happy to follow him. It was a match made in hell, as far as I was concerned. Ken had told me he was capable of a double life, years earlier. Was he living a double life now? I told him he needed to get away from Tony, and fast.

One day he came home visibly upset.

"Tony's refusing to pay the Khmer staff," he said. Ken hated the rich bosses who turned a blind eye to the suffering of the poor Cambodian workers. Now he was turning against Tony, and I couldn't have been happier.

"I can't believe he's making the construction workers continue building and sweating in this hot sun, and withholding pay."

"What are you going to do about it?" I asked. I hated Tony at this point.

"I took the computer. It's right here," he said. "I sent him an e mail and told him unless he pays the workers, I'll turn him in for embezzlement." Ken's phone rang. It was Tony. Ken agreed to meet with him, and gave conditions. Pay the workers, or Ken would give the computer to the aid agency. Tony was misusing hundreds of dollars on alcohol and women. And Tony wasn't paying Ken, either.

"When you play with fire, you get burned," I told Ken. "Tony's trouble, and he has been for a long time. You need to go down to the site and see if the workers are still gathered around the gate, or if they're getting paid. Get proof."

Ken went to the site but left the computer hidden and locked up in our house. He watched the workers getting paid by the Khmer accountant and talked with him, then returned the computer to Tony. Meanwhile, Ken was transitioning into doing election work in Cambodia.

Ken started getting a lot of positive attention around Phnom Penh. He became a savvy political analyst and election observer, and was well regarded in political circles. One day, he said he preferred ruling in hell (that would be Cambodia) to serving in heaven (the U.S.), and he planned to stay. Another time, he said he preferred being a large frog in a small pool. He was getting well-known, especially as we had been here since 1994. We were considered long-term expats now.

As for me, my lower abdomen hurt if I moved wrong. I was still convalescing, and didn't have much energy, although I worked at ACE fulltime. Teaching and working as a coordinator was easier than working for our business, driving around the city all day to talk people into buying ads. My second surgery in September, just three months after the emergency surgery in Phnom Penh, had taken its toll. I was tired, depressed, and I didn't enjoy Ken's nasty attitude and sullen behavior. I should have seen the writing on the wall.

In early 1998, Ken encouraged me to go home to the U.S. for a longer visit. I was pale, unhealthy, and weak from the events of 1997, and struggling with depression. When I got home, my mother visited from nearby Washington state, and was shocked at my appearance. I'd previously been slender, healthy, clear-eyed, and happy. Now, I looked old, had gained weight, and appeared miserable. My divorced parents went out for lunch—a rarity since they never talked-- and later admitted they'd discussed my very obvious depression.

When I flew to Calgary to spend time with Malgosia, who had

gone through the 1997 coup with us, I told her I suspected Ken was cheating, leading a double life. If it was true, he was lying constantly. She said, "Get out of Cambodia. You've got to get away from Ken and rebuild your life. You're still young." We sat on her couch sipping hot tea with honey. Her bright apartment was spotless, and flowers sat on the table.

I didn't feel young. I was exhausted, under considerable pressure, and knew I'd return to Phnom Penh and either save my marriage, or push it to the breaking point. I couldn't imagine life without Ken, but he had changed. He wasn't even friendly. It was all business, and most specifically, I was a worker for our publishing company and he was the boss. I wasn't the stay-at-home mom. Not hardly.

I flew back to Cambodia and began selling ads for Canby Publications, while also teaching at ACE. Ken coldly informed me that his mother was coming to visit, and asked me to prepare a bedroom for her. When she arrived in Bangkok, he'd take time away and tour her around, he said. I'd already traveled, so he expected me to work while he was gone. That was fair, but his anger was palpable.

In mid-1998, Ken began staying up all night, at least until 4 a.m. He had always been a night owl, but it had never been like this. I figured he dreaded another miscarriage and was avoiding sleeping with me. Around this time, an interim director arrived in ACE Phnom Penh, and the mood at the school changed dramatically. There were whispers between teachers that the interim director was checking on the credentials people listed on their job applications. ACE was cleaning house.

The interim director called me in. She said my bachelor's degree in English was insufficient. I needed to obtain a credential in teaching English to adult learners. She recommended The Cambridge Royal Society of Arts Certificate in English Language Teaching to Adults, the RSA CELTA.

In post-conflict Cambodia (after '97), our money was tight, and it was an expensive course. ACE would reimburse the course if I passed it, but a month away meant losing my salary, and the costs for the course, along with hotel and food expenses, would be about $3,000.00.

I talked with Ken. He was pretty reasonable about it.

"If you want to keep teaching, I'd say to take the course. The economy isn't great right now for selling ads, and I don't think you want to do that, anyway," he said. He was right: I had no interest in selling ads. The tropical heat and humidity of Cambodia, along with bouncing along on the back of motorcycles, was painful. I had to take care of myself. That meant saying no to selling ads.

Maybe if I could get Ken away from Tony, he'd shape up and stop cheating. He had to be cheating. Was he? All of this was like a looping tape of noise in my head. None of my decisions were good. I was depressed.

I made plans for the teacher-training course in Bangkok. I was excited to do this, as I loved teaching. Yet, I was dealing with the interim director at the school whose plan was to unseat me from my manager position as soon as I left. She wanted to put someone with a master's degree in my position. Knowing this was stressful, but ugly work politics just happen. I always landed on my feet. I decided to let the chips fall as they may. I had bigger fish to fry, as in dealing with my health and my failing marriage. I flew to Bangkok, and began the course.

On June 19th of 1998, I was done with the course, and it was my five-year wedding anniversary with Ken. It was only an hour-long flight from Phnom Penh, and he was flying to Bangkok. This would be an opportunity for us to have some fun. I thought, "We'll get through all of this. It's just a hard time." I got home from the grueling day at RSA school, and the front desk worker handed me a fax: *Happy Five-Year Anniversary! I love you very much, and we'll celebrate when you come home! I'm going to Prey Veng to do election observation work.* That night, everyone toasted to finishing the RSA class. I sat quietly. Five years of marriage had passed, and we were in trouble.

23

Meanwhile

When I got back to Phnom Penh, I found a young American guy with thick glasses in my office, with his feet on the desk. I stared hard at him until he put his feet down. He said he was doing my job now, selling curriculum. He gestured at the curriculum binders I'd assembled, ready for him to sell to clients. I tried to control my smirking. After the Phnom Penh coup (factional fighting), it was nearly impossible to sell anything. Aid dollars had dried up and floated away to countries whose governments weren't engaging in factional fighting in the street.

I held open the door, staring at the guy at my desk, "I have some things to do, thanks." I said. Until I heard from someone higher up the food chain, this office was mine. He looked confused and started to talk, then stood up and left. Wise choice. My heart beat hard, but I'd lost a baby and been through the coup within the same two weeks. I wasn't going to let myself be pushed around, and anyway, pointing his feet in my direction in Cambodia was considered rude. The top of the head is sacred; the feet are dirty. He had a lot to learn. Living in Cambodia for several years had changed me. I dressed modestly, ate with chopsticks, danced in circles with the Khmer people, and observed Khmer New Year. His feet on the desk!

The interim director, who'd orchestrated the workplace coup, had nothing to say. She didn't even give me the courtesy of a proper meeting, instead sending an assistant to deliver a teacher's contract to my office, which was about $300.00 less per month.

I was happy to be teaching again, away from the stress of trying to sell curriculum—especially since many businesspeople and NGO staff fled Cambodia after the coup. At ACE, I worked with a Cambodian counterpart, an intelligent man named Phalla. He could look at the schedule board—with plenty of Khmer and foreign teachers—and predict with accuracy who would call in sick next. The man had skills. He needed them for all the Monday morning absences.

In 1998, the drug ecstasy began flooding Phnom Penh. Plenty of head-banging was going on at the new rave bars, with people dancing nonstop to techno music. It was a constant party, and the Monday absences taxed the system. The staff was pretty much divided into four camps: young staff who partied, older staff who were responsible, older staff who partied and were accepted by the younger staff, and administrators. There were crossovers from every group.

One guy in his early fifties would hang out with the young staff and had trouble with his health. I checked on him at his home, and he let me into a dark apartment full of Chinese antiques and tapestries. I took fruit and expressed concern for his health. Later, I learned he was trying to maintain a reputation of benevolence, despite his attraction to "helping" young men who lived on the street, which eventually landed him in Khmer prison. "Helping them by fucking them," drily remarked Kris, a young male teacher from England.

Teachers partied a lot in Phnom Penh. Most were young and single. It was stressful living in a place with sketchy politics, but the nightlife was great. It was 1998, the year after so many events: the coup, my surgeries, bombs, and a plane crash in Phnom Penh in which a jet overshot the runway—all on board killed except a baby.

Several of us were on the riverfront of Phnom Penh, and the afternoon was open. Weather was a perfect mix of not too hot and not too humid, and we were drinking. The frangipani trees wafted perfume through the air, and the friendly elephant that walked the riverfront with his mahout came along. We fed him bananas. It was a perfect day.

One thing led to another. We found ourselves at a little bar on the south end of the riverfront with some musical instruments. Those of us who played turned the amps on, and began to sing. Others came in the bar, picked up on our energy and either joined in or left, some offended at our bad behavior.

After I went home to Ken, who was writing an election observer report and watching a movie, the partiers went to Happy Pizza, where the ganga was spread on thick, and they ate that. While gazing at the flag-lined waterfront with its fluttering flags for donor countries, three pizza eaters decided they'd cut down the Japanese flag. It had to be that one, and for no good reason. Joan, a young woman from Great Britain, urged the young men on. One thing led to another, and Kristopher climbed the pole and seized the flag.

As he descended, a mob of furious Khmer men grabbed him. He was messing with their country, their river, and their flags. Several of the angry men had clubs. At this point, if the Cambodian police hadn't come along, he may have been beaten, perhaps killed. Kris was glad to see the police. Now, he was carted off to the Khmer equivalent of hell, Cambodia prison.

In Cambodia, the inmates are crowded into filthy surroundings, tightly packed like sardines, and the care was horrible. Often they're stripped to their underwear. No one ever wanted to be put in Cambodian jail. The Khmer prison guards threw Kris into a filthy cell, and he passed out on the wet floor. He fell asleep with his cheek pressed to the cement, saturated with urine and sludge.

That night, his two partners in crime—Joan and other friend— went to the jail and turned themselves in. They felt guilty knowing he was suffering and they'd run away, but the male friend needed to dump the ecstasy in his back pocket. The jailers photographed the three perpetrators, and the local papers ran their faces. They were marched into jail, and local Cambodian news stations ran the video on local news.

The British embassy rallied and negotiated $300.00 release money per individual. Kristopher couldn't shake the incident, and left Cambodia fairly soon, but first he saw the doctor. He picked up a parasitic worm while passed out on the cell floor. The doctor removed the eight-inch worm, uncoiling the rubber band from its home in Kris's face.

Aside from incidents like this, 1998 was a quiet year with fewer foreigners around. Ken and I worked at keeping the publishing business afloat. Before he got an election-observing job with a U.S. agency, he wanted me selling ads for the *Siem Reap* and *Phnom Penh Visitors Guides*, along with the *Sihanoukville Visitors Guide*. I reminded him I'd just left a curriculum-selling position at ACE, and it was a bad time to sell anything in Cambodia. I was also still in pain, a point he didn't want to hear about.

"Ken, can you sell ads? I can write while you ride around outside in the sun. I'm tired of bumping around on dusty roads with busy traffic. My insides aren't good."

"No, I write the guides. I'm not going to write, do layout and sell the ads," he said.

"I know how to write, Ken. I was an English major, remember? Let's divide the work a bit." It had been eight years since we'd graduated from university, smiling at each other, and deeply in love.

He didn't like that suggestion. When I told him I was still struggling with pain, he said he was tired of hearing about it.

"Look, I have pain too, things I don't even talk about. We don't have the money for me to take care of myself," he said.

"I had no idea! What's wrong?" I asked.

"I'm not going to talk about it. We can't afford any more medical care. We've spent all our money on you," Ken said.

"Um, we wouldn't be spending money on me if it weren't for our pregnancies, right? It's not just me. It's us."

He walked away, angry. I recognized he was being unreasonable. I couldn't help what had happened. It's not like I wanted to have miscarriages and surgeries. He opposed me at every turn. Of course it was a stupid idea to ask him to help with selling ads. I needed to sell ads, because I was a financial burden.

He quit talking to me. Life at home became icy. I'd seen him do this before, but not to this extent. He hadn't experienced me saying no to him, either. Every day, I tried to talk with him, but "nothing's wrong" was the standard response. We just didn't talk. I'd lost a baby, and we didn't talk about that. Now, when he left the house at night and stayed out, we weren't talking about that.

"I'm going for a ride to clear my head," he said.

"Oh, nice. Want to meet at the riverfront?" I offered.

"No, I need to get a haircut. I'll be home in a couple hours." I knew all about the barbershop. Chris, his old military friend in Sihanoukville, went there to "clean out the pipes." Shave and a hair cut, ears cleaned, massage, and the female staff threw in a "happy ending," which in western parlance was a hand job.

After weeks of Ken's tight-lipped passive-aggressive communication, I couldn't stand it in our home any longer. I told the director of ACE I was leaving to sell the Canby Publication adverts again. She knew I was trying to salvage my marriage, and suggested I think hard about my choices. By saying that, she suggested I actually *had* choices, which I badly needed to hear. I was a mess.

I'd give things one last try with Ken. If I could somehow put all the broken pieces of our marriage back together, maybe we could fix things. Maybe we just needed a lot more time together. He seemed desperate to keep the company going, and I couldn't sell ads before. I still hurt from the surgeries. I wondered if I could sell ads again, now that it had been a while since the coup in 1997, the coup that was the beginning of the end of our marriage.

Around this time, Bell came to Cambodia to visit from Oregon. On the third morning she was there, she came down from the guest room upstairs and found me pacing, phoning a local hospital. Ken hadn't come home from his motorcycle ride the previous night. After a hospital worker said, "No *barang* here tonight," I told Bell that Ken and I were having problems.

She said, "Go back to Oregon. Your life is finished in Cambodia." Around 8 a.m., Ken wandered in. Bell left the room, going upstairs. She thought he was selfish, and knew there would be fireworks. I stared at Ken.

Ken said, "Wow, I can't believe what time it is. We've been at karaoke, and I went outside and it was light. There was a girl there who sang just like you."

I said, "Are you kidding? I've been calling hospitals, worried sick!" I wasn't letting him off the hook this time. Furious, I threw my coffee cup against the wall. It broke, and pieces of the cup flew everywhere. The coffee dripped down the white wall.

"Great," said Ken, pacing furiously. "Now I need to get a hotel so I can show our staff that you aren't the one in control." His eyes were red, and he reeked of beer and cigarettes. For the first time in a long time, I felt very much in control. He was lying, and I wasn't buying it. I have never in my life been so furious. It was right to be angry. I'd never in our relationship yelled at him or expressed anger. Never once.

"Do what you want," I said. "You should be worrying about what I think. By the way, if you don't think our workers are aware of what's going on, you're underestimating them." He went outside and kick-started his motorcycle. I went into the office and stared at the computer. My heart was jumping out of my chest. He appeared in the office door.

"I'm sorry. We just lost all track of time." He looked contrite.

"Ken, the problem isn't that you stayed out all night. You know what the problem is," I said.

"I'm sorry," he said. I felt ill, my stomach cramping and my mouth dry. I stopped just short of asking him if he was sleeping with prostitutes at that point.

"I've been indiscreet," he said.

The word "secret" is buried in the word indiscreet. He had secrets, and I was becoming someone I didn't like anymore, angry and suspicious.

24

In the Year 2000

I caught Ken telling half-truths constantly, but he accused me of jealousy. "What's your problem?" he asked, "You're acting so paranoid." All his affection for me seemed gone. We worked twelve-hour days with the publishing company.

Between losing the baby and postpartum depression, along with his emotional absence, I was a mess. New Year's Eve of 1998, we had a serious conversation. I suggested he'd strayed owing to the horrors of '97, and said I wouldn't hold it against him. He admitted that he'd slept with someone else, but just a few times. The surgery, the factional fighting—it had all been too much. He'd made a mistake. I told him I understood, but said, "If you do it again, I'll leave. You need to know that." We hugged long and hard, and kissed at midnight, ringing in 1999.

I'd hoped that the New Year would bring renewed happiness, but things didn't improve, and in fact worsened between us. I worked so much in 1999. We churned out about ten magazines, and I sold all the ads. I was up at dawn and in bed late. I never saw him at night.

He became icy cold. Y2K, the new millennium, approached. There was talk of computer problems, and air traffic control issues. Excitement was high in Phnom Penh. I was a bit unsure about our plans for that night. I worried he'd disappear, like he had on my birthday in September.

In September, we'd hosted a huge party for my fortieth birthday, on 9-9-99, at the restaurant RED with its brilliant crimson walls, modern art by Khmer painters, and Eurasian food. The owners, Marie-Claude and Raaj, were friends of ours, and great hosts. Some people worried that the hangers-on around the city would crash my party, but I wasn't worried. We wouldn't have a bar full of "ladies," and that alone would keep the riff raff men away.

The night of my party, Ken handed me a box with a beautiful ruby pendant, circled with diamonds. "It's amazing how reasonable prices are for jewelry here," he said, downplaying his beautiful gift. He always gave me beautiful gifts: wooden carvings, artwork, jewelry, silk fabrics. This night, he was in a good mood, and seemed happy to be with me. We went downstairs to the motorcycle, and Mr. Lim opened the gate. When I got on the back of his motorcycle, I was surprised at how good he'd gotten at balancing while I sat sideways. I hadn't ridden on his motorcycle for a long time. He drove too fast for my tastes, and we didn't have helmets.

I wore a long black dress I'd bought from Bliss, a boutique that belonged to an Australian woman, along with a black feather boa and red lipstick. When we entered, RED was packed, and the table was laden with flowers, bracelets, a golden Buddha statue, books, and candles. Dr. Scott was there, Glenn from the Walkabout, and teachers from ACE, even an older gentleman who'd recently landed his small plane in a rice paddy when the engine stalled. Marie-Claude greeted me warmly and put a gin and tonic in my hand.

For several hours, we partied. We ate chicken and beef satay sticks with spicy peanut sauce, along with lettuce rolls of shrimp, and a beautiful chocolate birthday cake. We drank from two kegs of beer, and mixed drinks with lime and lemon, and we danced. Ken disappeared halfway through. I was upset, but hid it from my guests. When he reappeared after an hour and a half, I was relieved to see him, and asked where he'd been.

"Just downstairs at Lisa's bar," he said. In fact, I'd kicked off my heels to run down the cement sidewalk an hour earlier. She sat behind the bar. Things were quiet, as my party with free food, beer, hard liquor, and dancing sucked up all the oxygen on the street. Lisa confirmed he'd been there, for ten minutes. So, he'd told me a half-truth. I didn't press him. My marriage was going south on Route 4, and I could do nothing to stop it.

For New Year's Eve, I bought a few yards of a sparkly, silver-sequined material and a pair of silver earrings. I threw a black jacket over my silver sarong and put on black heels. My hair was reddish-blonde from constantly being in the sun, and I put on peach-colored lipstick. We took the motorcycle down to the waterfront. I rode side saddle, and Ken was good at driving with me sitting on back. His motorcycle was a large dirt bike, and that helped too. We went out and had dinner, steak with sautéed vegetables and red wine. Then, we were off to the Heart of Darkness. Samnang, the owner of The Heart, opened it in 1993. It was the place to go then. We loved the owner, so we wanted to see in the New Year 2000 with him. Samnang was one of the most charming proprietors in the city, gracious and good-humored. Samnang was uninterested in taxi girls (and girls in general). His bar was filled with westerners and Asian people, and that was back in the days when great music played, not rave music.

When we got to the Heart, Ken started talking with a taxi girl named Wii, a flirty girl I'd I begged him to stay away from. She was trouble. She manipulated him, and her English was good. Generally, Ken liked skinny, straight-haired girls, but she was curvy with wavy hair. That all changed later when she developed a meth habit, and there were rumors she had *sidah*, the Khmer way of saying AIDS.

Ken and Wii played pool. I tried to play for a while, but I couldn't mask my annoyance. Ken and Wii were laughing and joking around, members of a club I wasn't welcome in. I put my cue against the wall and went to sit at the bar. It wasn't good. I didn't want to be angry that night, but it crept up on me. He eventually came to the bar.

"Ken, what's up with Wii? Did she know you'd be here?"

"I don't know. Why? The bar doesn't discriminate," Ken said. "It's a public place."

"You know that's not what I'm talking about. Should I go?"

"Do what you want." He stared at me coldly, then Wii yelled, "Your turn, devil!" He laughed and scooted into the little room. Ken's goatee had earned him a nickname. My heart raced. Should I push it, or wait? At midnight, Ken took many photos of me in the bar with Samnang on the other side. Glitters of confetti fell from nets on the ceiling. In the photo, I'm smiling, a pretty youngish woman in a silver sarong. In fact, I was so depressed. My feelings no longer seemed to matter.

We left The Heart and went to a dance club that was busy and loud. I didn't like the nonstop booming of rave music there, and neither did Ken. It was packed with Europeans, Australians, and Asians dancing and having fun. At 2 a.m., Ken asked me if I wanted to leave. I did, but we'd been drinking quite a bit. The ride to the club had scared me, which he knew. I thought we should take a cyclo home. He said, "That's crazy. Where do you think we'd put the motorcycle?" He'd started calling my ideas crazy the last few months.

I was depressed about losing the baby and feeling stuck in Cambodia, and he was putting me in the same category as his high school girlfriend. He called her crazy when he was ready to break up with her, he'd told me. My memory for conversation can be a curse, or a blessing. I was putting it together. He was distancing himself from me, which was especially hard since we lived on the other side of the world, away from my family.

"Ken, we have a pretty good buzz going here. Do you think you should drive?"

"Yes," he stared at me with a flat-line mouth, an angry look on his face. Had he brought me to this bar to just drop me off?

"Let's get a second motodop, and I'll ride with him, and you can ride the motorcycle. You won't have to deal with my weight on back. We can meet at the noodle stand." I was smoothing things over, but he was having none of it.

"I'm not going to stand around and talk. See you at home."

I followed Ken outside and watched him mount his motorcycle. This was a telling moment. I watched him jump the kick starter once, twice, and the engine roared. He looked both ways and sped off, never looking back. I was stunned.

Inside, foreigners, along with Khmers and Chinese, danced. Flashing lights and loud music were like torture. Surrounded by people, I was alone. How should I get home? I went outside and looked up and down the street. My feet were killing me, and I took off the high heels, standing barefoot on the pavement. A mildly drunken British guy meandered up.

"Hello there, I am so sick of Asian girls. Want to go for noodles? You look great. Have you been in Cambodia for very long?"

I couldn't blame him. I appeared to be alone. I thanked him and said I was married. Not that it mattered. He said goodnight and left. A cyclo pulled up, the rider high up on his bicycle with a cracked red vinyl seat in front. He hopped down from the high perch and I got in. He pulled the rickety vinyl cover over my head, obscuring me after I sat down. I tucked my handbag behind my back, so as not to attract thieves. He lifted and dropped his brakes a few times—click, click!—then began peddling back to my home near Olympic Stadium. I was there within fifteen minutes. I knocked on the locked metal gate, and heard Mr. Lim's flip flops padding to the front from his hammock near the back. He grinned, "Happy New Year, Madame Debra!" I thanked him. Khmer New Year wouldn't be for another four months, and that would be his celebration.

"Mr. Ken?" he asked.

"I don't know. Not here yet?" He shook his head no.

"Perhaps in thirty minutes."

He smiled, and I went in the house. I went to bed, relieved I'd made it home without being robbed.

About a month earlier, Ken had left a bar before I did, leaving me to go home on a motorcycle taxi. On the way back, I got mugged. Two young Cambodian men held knives to my throat, and my heart raced. While they rifled my purse, I said in Khmer "No good! I'm like your grandmother! your mother! your sister! Why are you doing this to me?"

I used everything I had to shame them, trying to sound like Polly and clucking my tongue. One of them reached into my bra and searched me thoroughly for money, taking time with grubby hands to pinch my breasts. Every woman I knew in Phnom Penh hid money under her shirt or in her bra. It kept us safe from the fast "snatch and grab," but not from being mugged.

The robbers left me with my jewelry, including a ruby ring set in 18k gold, as well as my thin wedding band. It was downright strange they didn't steal those items. They could have sold the gold. Khmers prefer the pure gold, which functions like money over there. Eighteen carat wasn't much to them. The pure gold was insurance. Car accident? Hand over the gold chain. Police issue? Hand over the earring. The robbers chatted with me, saying "You don't have any money? Why not?"

"I was going to get a thousand riels from inside the house when I got home to pay the moto," I said.

Often people in Cambodia did that with motodops and cyclos. I became human to the robbers, and they felt guilty. When I got home after being mugged, I told Ken, who was in the office smoking a joint. He was so mad he got the gun out of its hiding place, and prepared to jump on his motorcycle and shoot the robbers.

"Stop, Ken. What the hell."

"I know where they are. I'm going to take care of this."

"Wait, I'm okay. Come on. They're poor, stupid kids. Stop." He cooled down. This wasn't normal behavior. I was shocked and went to bed, after making sure that he was not going to commit a horrific crime. Ken wasn't so much angry with the thieves as at himself. He'd stopped caring about me, and Cambodia could be a dangerous place. I planned to go back to the U.S. for my annual visit home, and to make decisions. It was time to deal with the truth.

25

Cold Truth

In March of 2000, I went home to the U.S.A. for an extended visit. I went home every year to see my family and friends, but now that I'd become miserable in Cambodia, I needed to be away and think. It was obvious my marriage was tanking. Ken wouldn't go back with me to visit our family and friends, but he encouraged me to go.

Ken flew in to Bangkok when I returned to Southeast Asia. We met at Prasuri Guesthouse, where we hugged and smiled at each other, but I could tell something was wrong. He was quiet and seemed angry. He was aloof. He looked muscular, and was wearing a gold chain. He'd asked me to buy him some more modern clothes before I'd left for the U.S., and he was wearing the khaki pants with lots of pockets along with a black t-shirt. He looked younger.

We went out for a bite to eat at a restaurant on Khao San Road. Right after food arrived, he left the table, and was gone for half an hour. I felt anxious, and my heart pounded in my chest. Had something happened to him? Finally, he returned. He'd been to a barber and shaved his head. He didn't noticed I saw him putting his phone in his front shirt pocket as he walked back. He'd been talking with someone. I felt ill. I finished my coffee, and we went to our hotel room. It had been weeks since we'd seen each other.

"So, is everything okay?" I asked.

"Yes, it's fine."

"It's been kind of a long time since we've seen each other. Want to mess around?" I looked at him.

"Yeah, we could," he said. We made love, but it was perfunctory. It was enough for me to get pregnant.

When I learned I was pregnant three months later, I took test after test, seeing two pink lines and feeling elated. When I told Ken, he frowned.

"Seems like you had a good time back in the States. That baby can't possibly be mine," he said.

"We slept together in Bangkok, when I got back from the U.S.," I gently reminded. I felt the bottom fall out of my stomach. Why would he accuse me of sleeping with someone else?

"The timeline doesn't work," he said, moving toward the door.

"That was three months ago. I've never been unfaithful to you." I felt tears stinging my eyes, and sat down, dizzy. I put my head in my hands and cried. He was creating distance between us. He'd described this technique to me in early days when he left his first wife: go quiet, act angry, blame, and accuse. How could I have been so stupid to think he wouldn't also do this to me? I had to take care of myself. That was clear.

I made a fast appointment at Bumrungrad Hospital in Bangkok. I was praying that this baby would stick. Ken paced around miserably, and when I told him about some unusual pain, he grunted unresponsively. He said, "We can't afford more problems. I can't keep paying for your health issues. You need to sell ads. We have a magazine to get out."

"I've been selling since I got back three months ago. I've sold thousands of dollars' worth of ads," I reasoned. Nothing I said or did mattered to him now. I sold hard for two days, then I got on the plane. Ken refused to go with me. He needed to work, he said.

Boarding the plane, my lower abdomen tugged and cramped as I tried to put my small bag in the overhead. The year 1997 and memories of pain flooded back. I gasped and held on to a plane seat, dizzy. Then, Sharon was there.

Sharon, from New Zealand, was seven months pregnant and going for a checkup. She listened to my woes, and offered to go to the hospital with me. When we got to the waiting room, we were surrounded with pregnant Thai women. We went into the ultrasound room. The ultrasound technician looked and looked, and couldn't find an embryo. Then she said, "Ah, here is the baby." She pulled her screen around to show me, in black and white, the miracle of the beating heart, and the tiny fetus.

Tiny, but very much alive, it was growing inside the remaining fallopian tube. I stared, memorizing the image of the baby I'd never have. Another ectopic pregnancy. The technician turned the screen back toward her, and I begged, "A few more minutes, please, a few minutes." She cried, seeing my anguish. Sharon cried too.

Sharon followed me into the doctor's office, where we sat opposite a stoic, Thai surgeon. He stared at me, and simply asked, "Do you want me cut up and down, like this, or do you want me cut long across, like other cut?" He moved his hands as though giving a benediction to show me the cut options.

It had been just over two years since the surgery in Phnom Penh. I'd had a second "clean up" abdominal surgery in Bangkok as well. This was a third surgery, and a second baby lost. At that point, I broke down, crying as loudly as I've ever cried in my life. I had my head down on the surgeon's desk. I could do nothing to stop wailing. The misery of my broken marriage stood in front of me like a tower. I was utterly alone in my misery and felt as though nothing existed except the desk under me. Then, Sharon's arm went around me.

"Debs, I'm here." In her gentle New Zealand voice, she said, "We'll get you sorted. Come on."

She took over at that point. The doctor mentioned another surgeon at the clinic who used laparoscopy to do such surgeries, and perhaps I should see him. I called Ken after the appointment with the second surgeon. I told him about the ectopic pregnancy. I tried not to cry, but I couldn't help it. He cried too. Life in Cambodia had become miserable.

"I can't go through this again," he said in a quiet voice. How easy it was for him to say that. I didn't answer. I was working to breathe calmly and not bleed out. A nurse nearby waited for me, impatient. They wanted to prep me for surgery.

To Ken, I was inconvenient. Expensive. He was unsympathetic, because he was angry I was leaving. Even now, with the baby he'd fathered, he was absent. He had other concerns that didn't include me. All of these things occurred to me. Even with the tremendous sadness and fear, already I was hearing the voice. The voice of reason inside me, the voice of clarity. It said, "Hang in there. Stay alive. There's more to life. You don't have to live like this." I breathed. In, out. In, out.

"I'll be there soon," he said.

I hung up. The nurse took me to my room. The surgery would be at 5 p.m. I was admitted to the hospital, unable to walk anymore. Once again, medical staff said I'd hemorrhage and die. No, the baby couldn't be saved.

My friend Sharon went to the hotel to recover my small suitcase. I couldn't cry. I might hemorrhage and die if I got upset. I focused on breathing. I quit thinking. I cleared my mind.

In the operating theater, bright lights shone down from the ceiling. I was on a small gurney. I was alone in the room, except for a Thai nurse who occasionally came in. I finally fell apart. I started crying, and tears ran down my cheeks and into my ears. I could scarcely breathe as my nose clogged up.

The nurse announced the surgeon would be late. He was stuck in traffic. I asked for some medication to calm down, and I clasped my hands to keep them from flopping off the narrow gurney. She used a sheet to straitjacket my arms together, and administered an injection. Within a few minutes, I was so drugged up I couldn't move, but neither could I stop thinking. I stared at the light. I was 40 years old. I was losing my second baby, and in a miserable marriage. My husband had morphed into a robot, emotionless and cruel, over a two-year period. I had no way of wiping the tears, trussed up as I was. I focused on the light, staring. Over and over, I said *Hail Mary*. I wasn't Catholic, not at all. I needed a focus before I choked on my tears. I probably said at least 500 of those before the surgeon bustled in.

The tall, American-trained Thai surgeon looked at me, and said,

"What are you crying about? Sorry I was late! Not my fault!" When I awoke from the surgery, I was in a hospital room. It was dark. Sharon was there. She let me know things had gone okay. I'll never forget her. As a side note, Sharon cooked pots full of rice for the Cambodians who lived on the streets in Phnom Penh. She was an amazing humanitarian.

A few hours later, Ken arrived, and kissed my forehead. Sharon left. Seven months pregnant herself, she must have been exhausted. Ken and I talked briefly, and he went to sleep on the couch in the room. The next day, I was released to go to a hotel. The doctor said I needed to stay for a week. The surgeon had injected saline into the fallopian tube, which now needed time to dissipate and abort.

"We want you close to the hospital, in case it ruptures and you hemorrhage," said the surgeon. "Rest and try to take it easy."

I was afraid and sad. Would I see it? What was going to happen? The surgeon wouldn't say.

"Wear a pad and relax," he said. Highly unlikely I'd be able to do that. It was all pretty disturbing.

The day I got released, Ken wanted me to go shopping with him. He said it would be easy travel. In the taxi, I started having extreme pain. I just couldn't do it. He seemed irritated when I said I had to go back to the hotel. The taxi dropped me off, and Ken left to do his shopping.

When he returned, he said he needed to get back to Cambodia, and took a flight back that night. I dreaded postpartum depression, and knew it would set me back, but I'd made a promise to myself in the surgical room. I was going to get to the bottom of his cruelty, and figure out what was happening with our pathetic marriage. No answers would come from him. I had a strange obsession with figuring out what was happening. All the facts seemed to be right in front of me, but like with a puzzle, I couldn't put things together. I needed the absolute truth.

When I returned to Phnom Penh, he said I needed to go to Siem Reap immediately. I needed to sell ads, and we had a guide to publish within the month. Because I had been in the U.S., and then had the medical emergency, we had no time or money to spare. Work, or lose the business. I was floored. He had no compassion for the miscarriage.

My body was a mess. I remember being on the back of motorcycles on those dirt roads after the surgery. I felt my insides screaming every time the motodop hit a bump, and there were lots of them. I bled. I told Ken this, and he listened over the phone without comment, when he actually answered. I found a guy with a tuktuk, and I hired him to drive for me. The Cambodian message that played when Ken didn't answer his phone said, *the number you are trying to call is no longer in service, or is out of the coverage area.* I heard it again and again.

It was going to take a while longer, but I was not going to live like this. I would leave. Not yet. Soon. Moments of astounding clarity surprised me. I became aware of how much I loved Polly and Srey Mum. They looked after me. My friends did too. They gathered me up like a bouquet and looked after me. We had dinners. They asked about my health. Rumiko from Japan. Nina and Helen from Australia. Zinnie from The Phillipines. Meenakshi from India. These were strong, intelligent women who had travelled far to work in Cambodia. They told me about their lives, especially about their lost loves. They knew I'd lost babies, and they knew my marriage was a mess. That I was circling the drain, going down. My friends strengthened me by listening. I wasn't alone anymore.

26

*G*aslighting

At home in Phnom Penh, I was putting dirty clothes in the bin. I found a receipt for medical care for a woman in Ken's shirt pocket, a 22-year-old woman. I knew not to confront Ken. He'd gotten too good at staring me in the face and lying. Instead, I drove to our doctor's and got an accurate account. Ken had taken her in. It was a simple urinary tract infection, and she'd been prescribed antibiotics.

That night, when I casually asked Ken about the slip of paper, he said he'd picked it up to write a note on while at the doctor's office. He didn't know what it said on the front. He waved his hand, "No big deal. Scratch paper." When I told him I'd already been to the doctor's office —and knew that Ken had taken a girl in himself—he exploded, enraged.

"I overheard some girls talking, and I stepped up to help!" he raged. "I always try to help people, and knew I couldn't tell you!" I listened, watching his theatrics. Why couldn't he just tell me the truth? His girlfriend had a UTI. He'd taken her to our family doctor. I watched him curiously. I'd never seen someone so distraught, so motivated to conceal a lie. I knew the truth, obviously. Let's deal with it.

"I don't know why you think I'm sleeping with someone else! All I do is work," he said. I chose not to argue. I needed proof. Every time I found it, it wasn't enough. I could have just left, but I'd decided I needed to know. But how?

Ken flew to Siem Reap. I went to bed in Phnom Penh with the dancing apsara statue, carved wooden bird, and my goldfish in the bubbling tank to keep me company. I needed to fight my way out of this brown paper bag of depression and get to the bottom of Ken's cheating He denied it, and said I was crazy. Was I crazy? Maybe. I felt like I wasn't in control anymore. I'd been such a strong person.

Where had I gone? Could I get myself out of this mess? The answer was yes. Yes, I could. Yes, I would. I felt a surge of strength and determination. I didn't have to live like this any more. I might have to leave everything behind, but I could, and I would.

In the middle of the night, I woke with the realization that the phone company could help. They'd have call records. If I saw them, I'd know who was texting him constantly, when he heard the vibrating signal and slowly glanced up at me. I feigned indifference, and continued watching the television. He casually turned his phone over, then glanced back at me. Had I noticed? Why yes. Yes, I had. I stared at the television screen and wondered who was texting him, and why he was hiding it.

In the middle of the night, I knew what I had to do.

The next morning, I went to MobiTel when they opened, and requested the records, which they didn't typically give out. They knew me as their teacher and friend, and printed out two months' worth. At home, I taped the perforated records on the office walls, highlighting one phone number that appeared hundreds of times. The office walls turned yellow with the highlighting. Then I sat down with my phone and dialed the number.

A shrill Asian voice answered. This was a Vietnamese woman. Since neither of us spoke the other's language, we took the conversation to Khmer, which we both spoke well enough.

"What's your job?" I asked. In the background, I heard women laughing and chattering as she repeated my question. I could hear her mimic my voice, then there was a chorus of young voices and laughter.

"I collect garbage," she said. Everyone in the background laughed uproariously. My temper flared.

"I want to meet you," I said. "Tell me where you live." Things got quiet on her end when I told her I was the wife of Mr. Ken. Mistresses in Cambodia are terrified of wives, who sometimes throw acid in their faces. I'd never do this, but I was okay about letting her worry a little. I hung up, and within three minutes, Ken called.

"I hear you've been making phone calls," he said.

"Not as many as you have."

"I guess we should talk."

"No need to," I said. "And I'm crazy. You don't want to talk with me. I'm paranoid and delusional!" He'd been gaslighting me for months. I didn't know the word for it then, but I know the word for it now. Gaslighting.

Denying the truth.

Lying.

Using my depression against me.

Wearing me down.

Blowing up.

Telling me I was crazy.

"I'm sorry," he said. "We can fix this." I hung up feeling ill, but relieved I'd finally gotten him to admit everything. Polly came into the room and sat with me as I cried. A few days earlier, she'd beckoned me into his office.

"While you were in the U.S., Ken went to Sihanoukville," she said. "I found a photo of him with his sweetheart. Do you want to see?" She lifted his computer keyboard, and there he was with a skinny Asian girl and a group of friends. I stared at the photo and remembered something he'd said a few days earlier.

"Remember how everyone wanted to pose with photos with us in Vietnam?" he'd said. "I was in Sihanoukville, and everyone wanted photos with me posing with them." Preemptive strike. He thought I'd see a photo at some point, and was laying ground cover.

Most people have gone through breakups at some point. Ours was not typical. In fact, it was wretched. Ken met Kim through a bar run by thirty-year-olds in Sihanoukville, and she was a western guy's girlfriend's cousin. Ken and Kim were "fixed up." Theoretically, he would say, "Oh, sorry! My wife's in the U.S. right now, but we have a monogamous relationship." That did not happen.

Kim was from a brothel above the main road, or Whiskey-a-Go-Go, or Colaap I, or the port, the notorious "chicken farm" in Sihanoukville. Chicken Farm was a dismal stretch of dusty road with wood and tin shanties. Ken explained she wasn't in demand, and therefore wouldn't give him HIV.

I said. "So, you had slept with Kim when you got me pregnant in the year 2000. I was exposed to HIV, yes?"

"No. She doesn't have it."

"So, you were tested? Or she was? When? And there weren't any other women. Not one?" I asked. I didn't bother waiting for answers.

The woman my husband destroyed our marriage with was one of the ladies he had defended. Now it all made sense. I didn't blame her. Her parents, desperately poor, had sold her virginity to someone who came through the village. I can't judge her or any of the women trafficked around Southeast Asia. A minivan came to her village one day, and carted her away as if to take her to market. As if she were an animal to be sold. They were desperate people, doing desperate things. Maybe they believed the lie that the girls would be maids and restaurant workers. I don't know.

I considered staying in Cambodia. While I'd worked every bit as hard as Ken had to establish the company, he hadn't included my name on the ownership license of Canby Publications in 1996—a fact that he rather sheepishly explained. He'd been thinking ahead, realizing I wouldn't want to stay there. He was right.

It was time for action. I needed to rebuild my life.

27

Going, Going, Gone

In January of 2001, I began packing my bags. Just six months earlier, I'd lost the second baby. The physical pain was now gone, but I struggled with depression. At times, I snapped and yelled at Polly about the cockroaches lying upside down behind doors. That's where she left them. Then I'd cry in my bedroom so no one would hear.

One day, I used a shower towel that was loaded with red ants. They'd crawled on the towels drying on the cement wall outside. Red ants all begin biting me. I jumped back in the tub and sprayed down with water. They clung on, hundreds of them. Finally, I picked up a can of bug spray by one of the dead cockroaches in the corner and doused myself. Little ant heads were still attached, and I picked them off, swearing loudly. I was going to die of cancer. This bug spray was nasty stuff—*ShellTox* in the big yellow can. Polly got me the Tiger Balm. I was a wreck.

"I know how you feel," said Polly, "I was the same when my husband took a second wife. My heart was broken." She was so kind. I was the worst version of myself, and knew it. Ever the loyal wife, I didn't leave Cambodia until after Ken's forty-fourth birthday on February 25th. In the meantime, I told him I didn't want him sneaking around or lying. "If you want to go out, just go," I said.

So, he went out all the time. He'd say goodbye, then fire up the motorcycle and race away. My father emailed constantly to check on me. This was before the days of smartphones, and Dad had bought a computer when I lost the second baby eight months earlier. Dad wrote every day from the other side of the world in Oregon. He and my stepmom offered to help us with IVF so we could have a baby. This wasn't even in the realm of possibility anymore. In time, I'd tell my parents what was going on with my marriage. Not yet. I wasn't going to put my parents through the misery I was living with.

My chance to be a mom dissipated when I found the photo of Ken with the 22-year-old Vietnamese girl in Sihanoukville, her thick, black hair down her shoulders. I didn't think she was unattractive. She had sad eyes and high cheekbones, with large teeth. She was pretty when she smiled. I didn't hold anything against her. It was Ken who disappointed me.

It was hard to leave Polly and Srey Mum. Polly said, "If you stay, he will always think of her. If you leave, he will always think of you." As it turns out, Polly was right.

Ken and I were talking, finally.

"Cambodia's destroyed our marriage," I said.

"Well, no. I'd cheat in the USA like I have here too. It's a character flaw," he said. "It's not Cambodia."

"Do you think you're having mental problems?" I asked. I was gentle. I was concerned, although I was leaving. That was a sure thing.

"Depression for sure. I don't know."

He'd cheated on his first wife when they'd become financially successful. Maybe cheating on me was his way of bucking the system and being a rebel, something he liked. I was overthinking it all.

At one point, I asked him, "Why do you want to be with her?"

He said, "Why do you think?" He implied it was just a sexual relationship. I didn't think so.

"Our plan was to have a baby. It didn't work. Wasn't the next step IVF or adoption? What were you thinking?" I asked.

"I wasn't thinking, but I am now. We can fix this," he said. It was too late. Our marriage was broken beyond salvaging. Still, I faltered a bit.

"If you move back with me, maybe we could try?" I offered.

"If we have to leave Cambodia, we'll lose everything. Every dollar we've invested.. The USA--with its miserable people marching in lockstep—is not going to give us anything like we have in Cambodia," he said. "Rules and more rules, and taxes."

No money, no home, no autonomy, no retirement funds. He painted a pathetic existence. We had missed out on the American

Dream, and at forty-one and forty-four, we were too old to get back on track. I recognized his arguments were just a slippery slope of nonsense.

Ken corresponded with someone in the philosophy department at University of Oregon. He'd satisfied all of the requirements in 1994 with a 4.0 GPA, except for completing a section of the master's essays. He showed me emails from the department head. Ken shouldn't have left his capstone essay unattended, she said. Now, he'd need to fulfill the new requirements. Ken wasn't leaving Cambodia. Not ever.

He suggested we consider different options for our marriage. We'd already met one European man in Phnom Penh who lived with two wives, a young Khmer girlfriend and an older Chinese wife who spoke excellent English and appeared around town at art gallery openings. On occasion, we'd see the three of them out to dinner, the happy polygamist sitting between his old wife and his young pregnant darling.

"No, Ken. Not going to happen. How would you feel if I started bringing other people home? No."

One night, a young couple came and bought my piano. When they arrived, I played *Solace*, a song of Scott Joplin's. It's sad and slow. Ken listened. He'd never heard me play anything that wasn't upbeat.

I'd worked hard to acquire that piano. Phnom Penh didn't have such things readily available back then. I stood up from the piano bench and the woman gave me $800.00. I handed half of the money to Ken. They took the piano. Ken stared at me and didn't move. They took the piano, and he stood in the living room with his hands at his sides.

I left Phnom Penh in March 7, 2001 to return to the U.S.A. Ken asked me to spend a few days with him in Bangkok before flying out. When we were getting along, life was good, and now that I knew about his girlfriend and didn't seem angry, he wanted to spend time with me. I was in shock. The last time I'd been in Bangkok was nine months earlier, when I'd miscarried and had the surgery. I reassured myself, "Everything will be fine. It's time to leave." All I knew was I needed out. Out of Cambodia, out of Southeast Asia, and out of the horrible situation that Ken had hid from me for more than two years.

After the short flight to Bangkok, we stayed in The Dynasty Hotel near Soi 4. Ken liked the nightlife. Restaurants, nightclubs with the beautiful girls and lady boys of Bangkok, hookahs, dried framed beetle sets, rosewater from Iran, elaborate swords, pickled fruits, and chewy salted dried tamarinds were all readily available. Girls in tiny skirts stood in line with old white men to get little chicken drumsticks or pineapple. All the best and worst of Bangkok right there.

We spent three nights talking.

"There's got to be some solution to this," he said. "I think we can work something out. It's all my fault. I'm sorry. Please don't leave."

"So I can stay and sell ads for a company you didn't put my name on? Share you with other people? Stay at home while you're out all night? Live with someone who goes silent for months? Live away from my family, and go through horrible surgeries alone? No. Not a chance." I wasn't being sarcastic. This was my reality.

"Maybe Kim can have our babies, and we can stay together. She's going to get bored as a mother. She just wants money," he said.

"That's partially true, but you're now the goose that lays the golden eggs. And also, arranging for a surrogate mother is usually something a couple does together. You're not being fair to her."

"Maybe we just need to look at all of this differently. Maybe we need some time apart."

"I do agree with that," I said. "because the last few years have just about killed me." I was working at relaxing and breathing steadily. I wasn't going to let myself suffer any more. It had to be about me at this point. I'd already made him throw his hand revolver into the Tonle Sap, afraid of being left alone with it. I had to take care of myself.

Staying was out of the question. He'd had plenty of time and more than one warning. I didn't want to deal with being abandoned and neglected, overworked and taken advantage of ever again. I was hopeful, had hope, was hoping. Hope was the word of the day. I looked to the future, as the present time was a mess. It was all such a mess I got dizzy thinking about it.

In Phnom Penh, he and his friends drove their motorcycles around town with petite Asian women riding on back. He wanted to be one of the boys. Not possible with a wife from the USA, particularly one who'd lost two babies and was depressed and unhappy living away from family in Oregon.

I was fifty pounds too heavy to be sexy in Cambodia, with my British genes. There's nothing wrong with European genes, unless you're living in a country where European and American women are considered unattractive. I'd heard the western men in Cambodia calling European women buffalos for years. They still do. Apparently Ken had bought into that sentiment. I was done.

For three years, it was like I'd fallen off a cliff and struck sharp granite boulders all the way down. Who in their right mind would choose to live like this? I was going home to Oregon, the land of the Columbia River Gorge, the Willamette Valley, The Three Sisters Wilderness area, McMenamins Terminator Stout, Powell's Bookstore on Burnside, and Canby, my hometown. Life's not perfect anywhere, but I wasn't going to continue this charade. I wanted to be, as the Khmers put it, *sabay*. Happy. It was an option I'd forgotten about.

In Bangkok, we sat at an outside bar and watched the girls come in for their evening of dancing. This was a place Ken had spent some time, I realized. So many secrets.

"They stop at Buddha," Ken pointed out, "and pray for a good night, to not get hurt by anyone, and not get AIDS."

While editing our tourist guides to Cambodia, I criticized his description of "ladies" at this bar or that. He'd fallen in with the carousing men of Phnom Penh, and I reminded him that the old alcoholics with their young prostitutes used to irritate his sensibilities.

"Just say they're taxi girls," I advised. "Call it like it is. Or prostitutes. Sex trade workers. Why mince words?"

Of all the bars in Phnom Penh, the Martini Nightclub scene was the biggest spectacle. The bar had an outdoor screen for movies. Circular tables were outside with benches, and people from all over the city came in to get food, which was varied and plentiful. Food booths lined part of the perimeter of the outside area. Sandwiches were available, made with spam-like slices of meat on French baguettes with pickles and other condiments; barbecued chicken on sticks; little round meatballs, and all sorts of delicious Chinese and Thai food. Girls in beer sashes served cold beer and hard alcohol. There were *Angkor* and *Singha* girls in long silk dresses.

It was like a night picnic area under the tropical sky. Women were everywhere. The disco inside was an exciting and loud dancing scene, and Asian, European, and American men and their girlfriends danced there. We did too. The slogan of Martini's was "Hungry? Thirsty? Lonely? We've got everything you need!" That "everything" could include a girl to take home for the night.

Ken and I had a few meals there, watching the scene. I remember seeing one white guy walking around with an Asian woman riding on his hip, her legs wrapped around him. He carried her like she was a little kid.

"That's really disgusting," I said. Ken agreed. I had turned a blind eye to the men in Phnom Penh, like I'd turned a blind eye to the men in the woodworking shop back in Oregon. Now I lost patience with all of it. I went to the Walkabout Pub with Ken before I left Cambodia. An obese man with a bulbous, red-veined nose boasted that he could always make girls come. I got sick of listening to him, and turned to him, Ken whispering, "No, no! Don't talk to him! Don't!"

"So, just how can you tell?" I asked the old alcoholic, staring at him. At that point, I was done holding back my anger.

"I just keep a finger up their bum. You can tell when it twitches," he said, holding up his hand and showing me. My face twisted with disgust. I felt furious about the poor girls subjected to this horrible man and said, "Believe me, they're faking it." He yelled at me, and Ken pulled me out of the bar, "I told you not to talk to him. He's crazy." He seemed like one of the typical older expat guys to me.

Polly told me that Cambodian women were cloistered at home with the family until a marriage was arranged. That was traditional Cambodian behavior, taught to daughters through a set of rules called "chbab srey," rules for girls. Girls never appeared in immodest attire, and their formal costumes were made from the finest silk—long skirts that folded across the front and wrapped tightly around their bodies, with matching jackets nipped in at the waist. For school, young girls wore long skirts and white blouses. The women are raised to be soft-spoken and gentle, although they work as hard and certainly much harder to raise the children, cook and clean, and earn money. Asian markets are full of hard-working women.

Sometimes, Cambodian women worked in education or medicine, but more than one Cambodian woman told me that parents had forbidden her from learning to read and write, as parents suspected that literate girls would send love letters to potential boyfriends.

Many girls in the bars or brothels set their sights on foreign men. To land a husband was a huge social and monetary step up, and I know couples whose relationship sprang from nightclubs or brothels. Some of the hostesses (as they are called) just pour beer and work. In the '90s, the women pouring beer in nightclubs were often "working girls." Most lacked education and came from poor families. It was the only option.

I felt oddly serene. My last night in Bangkok, I went to bed with the carved wooden bird and the brass statue of an apsara dancer on the nightstand. In the morning, I stuffed them in my carry-on luggage. Soon, I was back in the U.S., lush green Oregon with Mount Hood just east of our farm in Canby. I put my wooden bird and the brass statue near my bed. The culture shock was huge for me.

In the U.S.A., people stared at me with suspicion. I'd apparently become too friendly while living in Cambodia. It was normal to smile and say hello to people there. In the U.S.A, restaurants were sterile and good food wasn't available unless you paid a lot. The fast food restaurants were disgusting.

Clothing I wore in Cambodia wasn't appropriate anymore, my airy tops and long skirts. My clothes from Cambodia looked oddly formal and feminine. I couldn't find anyone to speak Khmer with, and found myself muttering words and phrases to myself in Khmer language—*thank you, hello, black dog, rice with chicken. Go away, I'm sad, I'm not married now. I don't have any children.*

I dreamed I was on the riverfront in Phnom Penh. I missed Ken, the good version of him, the man I'd married. To counter the pain, I worked constantly. I got up at 5 a.m. to do yard work, and I didn't stop moving. The five acres around the house became perfectly manicured, like a golf course. I pushed around a wheelbarrow and shoveled bark dust. My father begged me to slow down. I couldn't.

Ken e mailed every day, talking about the business and giving me updates about what was in the *Cambodia Daily* and the *Phnom Penh Post*. How odd to get all of this attention from him now. It was as though we were happily married again, but I knew better than to trust his affection. To his credit, he sent me money every few months. He helped me transition back to life in the U.S.A, and I struggled for the first six months. Everything was hard. I'd been in Cambodia for years. At first, I couldn't get a job.

Eventually I was called for an interview at Nordstrom's, an upscale clothing store. I went to a group interview with a hundred people trying to get work and several interviewers. I told my interviewer anecdotes about my life in Cambodia—that I'd learned the Khmer language to sell advertisements. I stared him in the eyes and said, "Please, I need a job. You won't regret hiring me." I was the only person hired that day, he said later. When I started my new job, I stopped doing yard work for hours and hours, and riding for miles in the country on my old university bicycle.

I continued to edit for Canby Publications, as I didn't like just taking money from Ken. I got packets of text every week. Ken wrote me every day, and was kind. He sent packages of English-language newspapers from Cambodia, *The Cambodia Daily* and *The Phnom Penh Post*, so I could keep up with local news.

"Come home," he wrote. "We'll figure it out. I miss you."

I reminded myself that nostalgia shouldn't pull me back to Phnom Penh. I focused on the heartache—of being unattended in hospitals, left alone to suffer, and ignored. I reminded myself constantly of the hard parts, not just the pain of Ken's betrayal and lies and coldness, but the heat, the illnesses. My painful miscarriages. The twenty-two-year-old taxi girl who was now on my side of the bed. The silence in our home for so long. Move on, I told myself. Choose happiness. Look ahead.

Then, I met Jay. He was kind with a sense of humor, and we clicked. I told him about Ken, about everything. He bought me a small water feature for my bedroom when I told him I struggled to sleep without my goldfish tank bubbling nearby. He brought me flats of strawberries, and we went out for Mexican food. Life got better fast.

On September 11th, 2001, the terrorist attacks on New York occurred. Jay and I watched the people jumping from the twin towers, and all the misery and stress triggered a reaction that could only have been PTSD. Our first movie date, "Black Hawk Down," drove me into the lobby. The gunfire was too much like the July 5th incident in Phnom Penh. Jay started to understand me better.

In 2002, I went back to Phnom Penh. I missed my life there. Not so much that I'd go back, but enough that I wanted to go. I told Ken about Jay, who I lived with now.

"What's he like?" Ken asked.

"He loves nature, and being outside," I said. "He builds things with his hands, and he's a teacher. He's been married. He's got two kids."

"Good," said Ken. "I want you to be happy, but I still want us to grow old together. I miss you. I wish you'd move back."

"We can grow old as friends. Don't you think that makes more sense?"

"I don't know," he said. "I can't change things anyway." He looked miserable.

"Come on. You know why I left. You've got someone else now."

"Yes. But remember--you left me. I didn't leave you," he said. He honestly believed that.

28

*O*regon

The next day, we sat in the Foreign Correspondents' Club under the slowly spinning fans, and workers dried glasses behind the bar. Other westerners sat around, glancing at us. They knew who we were—we had established an extremely successful business in Cambodia and had lived there for years. Some gossiped about our break up as it played out around the capital city. I sat with Ken, talking about the publishing company, and reviewing plans for future projects. At one point, I mentioned how fertile the soil in Oregon was the previous year.

"So too was I, apparently," he said, in a quiet voice.

I felt the ground absolutely drop away. All conversation stopped. The room went silent. My heart seemed to stop. I looked at my plate of food and did quick math. His girlfriend must have gotten pregnant shortly before I divorced him. I felt a flare of anger. I felt a million emotions, none very positive.

At forty-two, I couldn't burden my boyfriend Jay with the news I needed to have a baby—fast—and that expensive fertility procedures were my only option. I did ask him if he wanted to have a baby, but he'd smiled gently and said, "I have two teenagers." *Stop thinking, stop thinking,* I told myself. I swallowed hard, and gripped the restaurant glass of ice water. I'm surprised it didn't break.

No second-guessing. I'd made the right decision in leaving. I had someone who loved me at home in Oregon. Graduate school would start soon. I wouldn't have a baby, not ever. This was the reality. Truth. I forced myself to look at Ken. He looked down, clearly uncomfortable. I'd come to Southeast Asia in 1994 and stayed with him in Cambodia. Built the company. He said himself that without my ad sales, there would've been no business. I did all the financial work while he wrote.

I'd waited for a family, and then nearly died trying to have babies. He disclosed his news with me about his pregnant girlfriend as though I wouldn't feel a stabbing sense of betrayal and pain. Right here in public with people looking on.

"So, how far along is she?"

"She's due in three months."

"Why didn't you tell me before I came?"

"I don't know. I wanted to see you. Maybe you wouldn't have come."

"I guess you're right." I took a sip of water and tried to stay composed. I looked up. People had turned in their seats to watch us, and turned back around. Later, a friend in Cambodia admitted the community—a Greek chorus of sorts and always watching--worried I'd decided to return to Ken. Not long ago, they'd rallied around to tell me he was buzzing around town with the Vietnamese girl on the back of his motorcycle. Half a dozen of them had told me. Even Polly.

After a few minutes, Ken paid. We went to the motorcycle and I sat on the back, and cried a few tears, all the while thinking, *move on. And don't let him see you cry.* We rolled along the riverfront of the Tonle Sap. We passed the many-storied building of an old hotel, dilapidated and filthy, with clothes lines across the top floors. Ken's friend Wii had lived in one of them. I made myself calm down. By the time I got off the motorcycle at Ken's apartment, I was done being sad. I'd chosen to leave all of this, and in another week, I'd be on a plane home to Oregon. *Come on,* I told myself. *What did you expect to find out?* Of course he was having a baby with the kid from Vietnam. It was the next logical step.

Grief wasn't going to be a long odyssey this time. Grieving my brother had taught me a lot. So had all the misery in Cambodia. I'd look ahead, not back. No anger, no denial. I didn't need to remind myself of Ken's wrongdoings. I wouldn't move back to Cambodia and share Ken and Kim's babies, which he offered. I wouldn't be bitter. I could look at the blue Oregon sky and feel content. The next day, I took the money I'd earned editing our magazines and bought matching rings for Jay and me. I reminded myself I'd rebuilt a life in the Pacific Northwest, away from the traffic and smog of Phnom Penh. I loved the provinces, but I'd never loved the city. I had a different home now, anyway. I told Jay everything when I got home. Jay was pragmatic, "You've got to move on. That's all we can do. Be happy and live well. I love you. We'll be fine."

By the time Ken and Kim had a second child, I'd come to terms with it. I'd built a life with Jay, and that helped. I visited Cambodia, and held Ken's baby in my arms and played with the older child in the swimming pool.

When Ken and Kim and their children came to Canby, Oregon in 2009, we took them to Silver Creek Falls, had a picnic and went hiking. They stayed in our home. By that time, Jay and I had a relationship so solid nothing could shake us.

Ken still lost his temper frequently. He fretted that his daughter wouldn't eat. He fussed and complained that her failure to thrive would be worsened with our food. She was tiny, but she ate more than adequately. Ken's girlfriend cooked rice at our stove and monitored its consumption closely. My husband Jay, a father of two, didn't understand the myopic focus on the kids. Ken asked me to drive to a KFC for a bucket of drumsticks for the oldest child. Ken said, "I'll do whatever I need to do to feed my children." Okay, then.

As I drove them to the airport the next day, Ken fretted he'd lose the publishing business if I got them to the airport late. The lecturing lasted the forty-minute drive, and had me so upset I worried I'd overshot the exit. They got out of the car at the airport, and I gave them a quick hug goodbye, adrenalin making me jumpy. I was relieved to get home to Jay and peaceful silence.

I couldn't maintain the anger and sadness I felt when I left Cambodia in 2001. It would have killed me. Ken and I became friends. I kept up with deaths and marriages in Ken's family, and he kept up with mine. He always asked about my parents. I asked about his, too. We were growing old together, but on my terms. He accepted that in time, and I knew he had a happy life with Kim and the children they had. We kept the best part of our relationship, and I felt no anger or bitterness. I'd decided not to.

Recently, I was talking to Bell. I asked her, "Why was I able to become such good friends with Ken, after everything that he did? I miss him still, and it's so strange to me. Most people who break up just hate the other person. Especially considering the circumstances."

"You loved him, and love is complicated," she said.

"Yes," I said, "to love someone, to see them up close under a microscope, you're going to see those imperfections, the cracks in the armor. And some cracks are so huge."

"And you love them anyway. You look past the wrongdoing," she said. "But if it's bad enough, you leave. It's good that you left, but you found a way to continue a relationship somehow." Bell was right, as always. The woman who'd seen me through my brother's death understood me.

I tried to see things from Ken's point of view. He was a difficult person, which he'd admitted early on. He told me his past, and I listened, but I didn't take it as a warning. And I'd loved him, although he vacillated. Mean, gentle, mean, gentle. After the coup and the baby lost in '97, he'd deserted me and become silent, then permanently aloof. A constant anger on the back burner, simmering quietly. His world was destroyed when I nearly died and couldn't have babies. His plan was ruined, and he cracked under pressure. As for me, I was a damn good wife, and I left because I had to. This was for my benefit entirely. He wanted me to stay, but it would have been an unhappy life. I was finished with being unhappy.

I was by no means perfect. Hadn't I retreated into work rather than confront our issues? I asked Ken shortly before I found out about Kim if he was happy.

"I'm not unhappy," he said. That was so hard to hear him say. Maybe Ken just wanted to experience joy again with a young girl. Maybe Ken wanted to have kids, as his alcoholic cousin said when he called me home in Canby at 2 a.m.

"Face it," he railed. "Ken wanted progeny! You missed the window, and you couldn't have kids. That's what broke up your marriage."

Thank you, cousin of Ken. Now *that* relationship I began ignoring.

How did I get through my break up with Ken? I wish I could say that living in Cambodia for years steeped me in a philosophy of *annica*, impermanence. Nothing lasts. Everything changes. I've seen so much death and loss nothing surprises me anymore.

This is closer the truth: I chose happiness, and moved forward. Get busy living, or get busy dying. I chose life. It was hard work. I dealt with my grief through hard physical labor. I simply worked myself into the dirt. I rode thirty miles a day on my bike. I did yard work for my father from dawn to dusk with shovel and wheelbarrow. I wrote lists and lists of reasons I'd left. I had to remind myself of why I'd plucked my miserable backside out of Cambodia.

The culture shock was overwhelming. Oregonians looked away when I smiled at them. Not only that, I'd lost a baby the previous year. I filed for a divorce and cried in the courthouse bathroom when it was granted, sitting on the tiled floor until I could stand again. Rebuilding my life was hard. It took longer than I'd like to admit, but I moved forward. I put mind over matter. I would find my way again, I told myself. I had to believe that.

Finally, I forgave Ken and when I did, I felt such relief. Online, I saw a quote attributed to Buddha. It goes like this: "Three things cannot be long hidden: the sun, the moon, and the truth." The truth for me is that Ken and I became friends. Some exes can't pull that off. We did. And that quote above isn't really from Buddha, by the way. Not entirely.

Now I live in Oregon, on the farm with tall cedars and mallard ducks on the pond. The blue heron flies in and drops blue-gray feathers while our cats sit on the bank and watch him. Jay and I hold hands and take walks, happily arguing U.S. and world politics, and what might be for dinner.

We've been married for fourteen years, together for eighteen.

His kids have grown up, and we have three grandchildren. We've tucked our parents into their resting places, and have experienced love, change, and loss--together. We're growing old. I'm fifty-nine now. And did I learn to deal with loss? For the most part, yes.

My brother would be fifty-eight years old, but he lives in my memory as an eighteen-year-old. Forever Young. When I think about him, it's mostly the happy memories. The way he played drums on the dash of the '68 Mustang, the love he had for all of us. The light peach fuzz on his face when he was eighteen. His baby blue eyes, and his laugh. I smile when I remember him. The hard memories I've learned to block. I learned to do that in Cambodia, my home on the other side of the world.

Over the years, people have asked me if I missed Cambodia. Here's the truth. Those who've lived in Cambodia remember the lilting music, the incense, the lazy fan overhead in the FCC, and the wide flowing Tonle Sap, a river that changes direction each year, a natural event that the Cambodians love and celebrate. I remember the monks in orange robes, and the magic of the temples in Siem Reap; the graceful dancers, with beautiful fingers that curve back and resemble the eves of the palace. I remember the happy brown eyes of Cambodian children. I miss Cambodia every day. I don't second-guess my decision, though. I chose happiness, and that's what I got.

"Ken's body is missing." Nothing could have prepared me for those words. Ken's brother called me December 7th, 2016 to tell me Ken had fallen from a boat while disembarking. A splash was heard, and people ran to see, but the sun was setting. Cham fishermen searched in boats. I sat on the floor of the office, phone in one hand and a newborn baby in one arm. It was 9:00 a.m. in Puyallup, Washington, and I held my grandson. I hadn't heard Dale's voice in years, but I recognized his courteous mid-western tentativeness.

"Have you talked with Ken recently?" he'd asked. Indeed I had. Their mom was dying. I'd just forwarded Ken a photo of her in her hospital bed, with a bright bouquet I'd sent. It cheered him to see her smile.

"You've got to get home fast," I'd told Ken.

"I've got tickets," Ken said. "I'll be there December 10th. I'm just getting a few things done around here, and I'll fly out on the 9th." While in the U.S., he would buy Christmas presents for the kids. His voice cheered at that. He'd be there for his Mom's passing, or one of his brothers would.

In the last year, Ken and I had shared discussions about life, love, children, regrets, and friends in Cambodia. In hindsight, it was more like closure than simple conversation. He texted, "I'm thinking more and more about retirement. Did you know the average mortality for expatriate men here is 58?" I texted back that I didn't know what I'd do without him in my life. What a strange thing to say. Oddly sentimental. Where had those words come from?

After I'd left Cambodia in 2001, the meanness inhabiting his body vanished, like his Khmer teacher's ghost during the Khmer Rouge years. He was himself again, the kind version. He opened up to me and we became friends. That is, after I biked thirty miles a day for several weeks and landscaped a ten-acre lawn. After I worked eleven years of our relationship out of my system.

Ken's children made him a better man, and I told him so. He was often tired, but worked relentlessly to provide for them. The drivers and nannies took care of the children, and Kim came and went as she pleased. Ken built her family a big house in Vietnam, and tried to keep a lid on her gambling habit.

When Ken's body was found, Kim telephoned me as she walked along the riverbank on Koh Pich as people led her to him. She worked to include me, a kindness. She began crying. She needed to hang up, she said. Later, I saw photos. His black shoes floating up in the water. It was him.

It took twenty-four hours to fly to Phnom Penh for his funeral. Kim asked me to look through items from his safe. Alone in his office, I sat in his chair, looking at what he'd surrounded himself with. Gifts from our years together covered the walls and filled the shelves--the red Russian nesting ball I'd put his wedding ring in so long ago. The framed apsara angels from Angkor Wat. Small souvenirs from Marble Mountain in Vietnam. He'd surrounded himself with mementos of our years together. Photos of Kim and the children sat on his desk, which made me smile but also made me sad. They needed him. What would happen now?

In his safe were photos of us reading wedding vows to each other, and a neatly handwritten letter. He wrote words I'd never heard him say. Private things I won't write here. He missed me, the letter said, and he regretted hurting me. It was as if he knew I'd be sitting in his chair, in his office, right there. Sure, he knew. He had prepared meticulously for this very situation. I cried, a fast monsoon, but reminded myself it had been fifteen years since I'd left Cambodia. I wouldn't waste years as I had with my brother. I'd learned how grief is supposed to work.

I tied red yarn on my wrist at the funeral for Ken. I delivered a funeral speech, and cried hard when the mourners marched around the crematorium several times, with music playing. I gave grief its due, and then boarded the flight back to Bangkok. I was exhausted, and got on the plane in Cambodia wearing sandals. In Bangkok, I boarded the international flight for Los Angeles. When the flight attendant reached for the box with Ken's urn, I held it tightly. She glanced at the writing on the box and understood.

"One moment," she said. I saw her talking with the other workers. After they talked, she ushered me up to business class, and put me in a seat with Ken's urn in his own seat, buckled in. It was hard to believe twenty-two years earlier, we'd flown to Bangkok together. Now, I escorted him back. At LAX, a woman saw me shivering at the airport and gave me a pair of wool socks. The kindness brought tears to my eyes. She and another passenger sat near me and talked, comforting me with their voices. I sat with the box, wrapped in export papers with stamps all over it. In Oregon, Jay stood at the gate, looking anxious. He wrapped his arm around my shoulder.

"I'm so glad you're home. These last few weeks have been

hard."

Jay had helped me grieve the loss of my marriage back in 2001. I'd talked him through the hard work of forgiving his ex. Holding on to anger never helps, especially with kids involved.

"I got you something," he said. He handed me a small box. Inside was a sapphire ring.

"Jay. I love it. Thank you. Why did you buy me this?"

"Oh, just because." He wheeled my luggage, and took the box with the urn from my arms, "I think I know what this is."

Jay had seen me through the deaths of both parents, both stepparents, and my dear friend Sally. Now, we were losing his mom to Alzheimer's. It was a relief to see Jay, his baseball cap a little crooked and a worried look on his face.

"Are you hungry?" he asked.

"Starving."

"I got you a roasted chicken and some grapes. Let's get you home and fed. Then you can sleep."

I told Jay everything. How I'd gone to the riverfront to see the boat, and to figure out how Ken had fallen. The letter I'd found in the safe. The wake on the boat Ken fell from. The burlap sacks of ashes we threw by handfuls into the Tonle Sap. I showed him the video of Ken's friend scrutinizing the ashes, then eating some. A friend had grabbed my phone to record the moment, so it was a surprise.

"We can talk more tomorrow," he said. "But you may have to make the chicken soup yourself."

"What chicken soup? What are you talking about?"

"You know, in 100 days. When you're totally happy again." Jay loaded my luggage into our car. Then, we went home and went to bed, the light of the moon coming through the window.

DEBRA GROVES HARMAN

These were the first three covers of the first three guides we published. The Sihanoukville Guide top left was the first of all the magazines. It was at press during the coup of 1997.

The guide on the left features Srey Mum on the cover, a very young girl in the late 90s.

I took all the photos except for a few on the Siem Reap Guide. An aerial photo left and center was taken by a French man who had an ultra light!

At Ken's house in
Phnom Penh,
Cambodia 2002.
Deb and Srey
Mum (Socheata).

Photo by Ken
Cramer.

Top: Ken Cramer at Angkor Wat, 1995, photo by D. Groves Harman.

Bottom: Ken Cramer at Angkor Wat, early 2000s, self-portrait. This is perhaps Bantey Srey, "temple of the woman."

Author Debra
Groves Harman at
Angkor Wat, Siem
Reap, Cambodia in
1995. Photo by Ken
Cramer.

Ken in his office, 2002. Photo by D. G. Harman. I took several photos of him on this day. This was my favorite. In three months, his first child would be born, and he became a great dad.

Bayon Temples at Angkor Wat, Siem Reap, Cambodia. 2008.

Angkor
Thom North
Gate
entrance.
Angkor Wat
Temple
Complex.

2008.

Polly in Phnom Penh, Cambodia, 2002. Photo by D. Groves
Harman.

Magnificent Angkor Wat Temple, 2002

Acknowledgements

Thank you deeply to the people of Cambodia. I'm especially hopeful that some of my students will remember me and send a note.

I'm grateful to Bernard Krisher and Deborah Krisher-Steele, who granted permission to reference The *Cambodia Daily* when I confirmed incidents and dates. Thank you to The *Phnom Penh Post* online sources, *Cambodia Expats Online*, and *Khmer440*.

Assistance came from many sources, including Natalie Gasper, Jay Harman, Bill Herod, Leslie K. Loofbourow, Brian Paul (*Canby Media* in Cambodia), Jill Rothenberg, Susan Shapiro, and Bill Siverly. Thanks also to Philip Cogan, author; Dr. Bunkeng Tuon, author; and C.B. Bernard, author, for their help. Kendall Willis designed the cover, and Ian Eilert assisted with the apsara silhouette graphic.

Thank you to friends from Cambodia days, especially Helen Cherry, Dr. Gavin Scott, Malgosia Bednarek, Raaj, Richard Tracey, Bill Irwin, Tom Hricko, Pech Arunn, Symond Russell, Lizzie Neil, Marie-Claude Ayotte, Bert Hoak, Mdme Lim, Sharon Beattie, Paul Mahony, Heidi Flugstad, Julie and Jerry Mobbs, staff at ACE Phnom Penh, and my students in Sihanoukville and Phnom Penh, Nina Weir, Meenakshi Negi, and Rumiko Taniguchi. Thanks to Jamie Lambo and Jason Roberts for advice with writing Anglicized Khmer language. I'm grateful to Jay, Heather, Jaclin, and Jon for reading and commenting on my creative nonfiction. Also, to my friends who have supported my work, including Lowell Brown, Robert Mulkey, John Larson, Vicki Woolhiser, Bronwyn Carnegie, and Michele Summerlin. All photographs are by Debra Groves Harman unless otherwise credited. Thank you to the magazines and journals that have previously published my writing, as follows:
A portion of Chapter 4 was published as *FTO Star* in "The Write Launch," January 2019; an earlier version of *Sihanoukville by the Sea* was published in "The Nasiona," Issue 1, August 2018; an essay entitled *Mary and Goldfish* was published in "Miracle Monocle," Issue Twelve, Spring 2019 and is similar to chapter 25.

Bibliography

The Cambodia Daily and *The Phnom Penh Post* deserve strong recognition for their work, especially during the 90s when many of us relied heavily on the English-language newspapers, before the days of online news. The books and articles listed below have also been helpful.

Brinkley, Joel. *Cambodia's Curse.* New York, NY: PublicAffairs, 2011.

Garella, Rich, and Eric Pape. "A Tragedy of No Importance." *Mother Jones*, April 15, 2005. Accessed March 20, 2019. https://www.motherjones.com/politics/2012/11/cambodia-war-khmer-sam-rainsy/.

Grace, Kelly and Eng, Sothy. "There is No Place for Chbab Srey in Cambodian Schools." *The Cambodia Daily* 25th Anniversary Issue Online. 9 June 2015.

Smith, R. Jeffrey. "FBI Points Finger in Cambodian Attack." *The Washington Post*, June 29, 1997. Accessed March 20, 2019. https://www.washingtonpost.com/archive/politics/1997/06/29/fbi-points-finger-in-cambodian-attack/.

"Summary UN--Cambodia UNTAC Background." UN--Cambodia UNTAC Background. Accessed March 20, 2019. https://peacekeeping.un.org/mission/past/untacbackgr1.html.

Willemyns, Alex. "Making of a Strongman: In July 1997, Hun Sen Took Full Country of the Country--and His Party." *Phnom Penh Post*, July 5, 2017. Accessed March 20, 2019. https://www.phnompenhpost.com/national-post-depth-politics/making-strongman-july-1997-hun-sen-took-full-control-country-and-his.

Hiking the West Highland Way in Scotland with husband Jay Harman in 2016.

Debra Groves Harman taught high school English for many years, and is now a substitute teacher. She enjoys walking the *Camino de Santiago* in Spain, working on the farm with her husband Jay, and playing in the Jesse James Band with her musician friends.

Her undergraduate degree is a BA in English literature from University of Oregon, and she has an M.Ed. from Portland State University. Her creative nonfiction appears in several magazines, including *Miracle Monocle, The Write Launch, The Nasiona, Not Your Mothers Breastmilk, OJAL: Open Journal of Art & Letters, Two Sisters Writing and Publishing*, and more. This is her first book.

Sometimes you can find her at Silver Falls State Park, working as a Trail Ambassador. You can also find her on Twitter debragrovesharman@harmanygroves or drop a note via e mail harmanygroves@gmail.com

Made in the USA
Middletown, DE
09 July 2019